VOCABULARY OF A
MANAGER

VOCABULARY OF A MANAGER

POWERFUL PHRASES to Manage Your TEAM EFFECTIVELY

Charles Holding

Published by
Rupa Publications India Pvt. Ltd 2022
161-B/4, Gulmohar House,
Yusuf Sarai Community Centre,
New Delhi 110049

Sales centres:
Bengaluru Chennai
Hyderabad Kolkata Mumbai

Copyright © Rupa Publications India Pvt. Ltd 2022

All rights reserved.
No part of this publication may be reproduced, transmitted,
or stored in a retrieval system, in any form or by any means, electronic,
mechanical, photocopying, recording or otherwise, without the prior
permission of the publisher.

P-ISBN: 978-81-291-4548-2
E-ISBN: 978-81-291-4934-3

Twelfth impression 2025

15 14 13 12

The moral right of the author has been asserted.

Printed in India

This book is sold subject to the condition that it shall not, by way of
trade or otherwise, be lent, resold, hired out, or otherwise circulated,
without the publisher's prior consent, in any form of binding or cover
other than that in which it is published.

CONTENTS

Preface *vii*

1. Nitty-Gritty of Conversation — 1
2. What Works Best at Work — 14
3. Lowering Temper — 29
4. Winning Diplomatic Battles — 43
5. Put Yourself in Their Shoes — 58
6. Please, Sorry, Thank You! — 73
7. Not All Speak Alike — 84
8. Talking After a Long While — 94
9. Using Communication for Impact — 109
10. Respect All Views — 124
11. Bragging is a Big No-No! — 141

PREFACE

Imagine. Imagine sitting in a coffee shop with a bunch of close friends from school, six years down graduation. This is a reunion after years. There are many things to catch up on, many stories and tragedies to be shared. Conversations would follow effortlessly with each cup of coffee being refilled. Before any of you realize, hours would have gone by and there would still be laughs left to share.

Now imagine another set-up, of a slightly different nature. You are meeting a potential employer for the first time in a professional gathering. A topic is what you are on the lookout for, to initiate a conversation with the person. It is not possible to approach casually; you are hell-bent on creating an impactful first impression. The atmosphere is bound to become a little tense.

In both instances, communication works differently. While it hardly needs an impetus in the first one, a well thought out and calculated move needs to be followed while initiating a conversation in the second example. However, both have something in common—the need to start a conversation, the need to communicate. Without this basic criterion, there would be no friendly banter taking place or you wouldn't be introducing yourself to your potential employer. What's also similar in both situations is the basic communication etiquette, without which, fetching a response from the other party would become difficult; a set of questions are posed back and forth to which answers are given. A simple rule of communication is followed and fulfilled.

If communication served a singular purpose, there wouldn't have been the need for this book or any other, in that case. Be it your professional, personal, or social life, the way you communicate with others always plays a huge role in shaping your inter-personal and often intra-personal relations.

When the world was first hit by a pandemic in 2020, the need for better communication among world leaders and with one's own countrymen became unprecedented. While countries communicated with one another on how to tackle the spread of the virus, individuals too, engaged in helping out each other. All of this remained possible following the need for better communication, following the need to stay connected in these tough times. With the world now emerging out of the troubled waters, and people slowly returning back to their normal lives, the need to develop better interpersonal relationships has been like never before. This heavily relies on one's ability to decipher verbal and non-verbal aspects of communication. Your thoughts, emotions and ideas should be conveyed exactly the way you perceive them first in your mind. Hence, becoming cautious about choosing the right words and portraying them through correct body language is imperative. Communication is also a must for resolving conflicts and misunderstandings of any sort, be it amid two nations, two families, or two individuals; the purpose remains the same, by and large.

Communication does not and cannot be inclusive only of the said words; it is also influenced by the way you present the same. Being able to mask or control your rising temper in an argument, winning diplomatic battles, being able to negotiate, being open to acceptance of new ideas, understanding what works best in a workplace conversation and in a casual one, being polite and considerate also make for impressive communication skills. The sender, receiver, the channel through which the message is sent, the message itself, and the feedback received form a chain of a proper conversation.

This book will take you on a journey of how to hone your communication skills. You may turn over to any chapter, as and when you want, or delve into the book chapter-wise. There is no one correct way to make the maximum utilization of this book. The content is in a conversational style and often chatty in nature. It might be like having a conversation with your friends and families—a leisure activity.

Components of some chapters might end up overlapping with those of another, but the title is such that it can be hardly helped.

I

NITTY-GRITTY OF CONVERSATION

'The true spirit of conversation consists in building on another man's observation, not overturning it.'

—Edward G Bulwer

The way you strike a conversation with another person or in a group conveys a lot about your persona. You can be taken for an imposing person or a considerate one only on the basis of the words you choose and the way you present them. Being wary of inappropriate words and understanding what a real conversation entails becomes imperative to a person, especially to someone who aspires to become a leader one day; what is a good leader without good communication skills.

Your ability to hold a conversation and involve the other is also an imperative part of good communication skills. What needs to be remembered is that conversation always involves two active parties and if either goes passive, it would instead become a monologue—for the speaker, by the speaker. Here are 10 ways in which you can ensure that your communication skills enable you to engage in a meaningful conversation.

Use Shorter Sentences

Stick to the usage of shorter sentences in your conversation. Talking to a colleague or a client should not turn into a speech. Convey your ideas in a precise and crisp manner, such that your point is easily conveyed to the listener without creating any scope of boredom or avoidance. In case of important conversations—ones which can act as determiners of your future—come prepared with certain points in mind beforehand. Avoid fluff words that might cause your audience to lose interest in what you are talking about. This will help you from wandering off the topic.

Break your sentences into smaller units that are easier to process. Shorter sentences are known to create punch and strike a chord with the target audience. They can be used effectively in speeches and presentations to create a sense of haste and urgency which is often needed. They help you present clearer ideas and leave no room for confusion or the possibility of conflict—both of which can land you in trouble.

Everybody's attention span has drastically reduced and this needs to be kept in mind during conversations, especially with ones who are important to you personally or professionally. Express your idea in the least complicated way and with the usage of minimum words. It would save you time and energy, and the other person too would be grateful.

Read for Better Vocabulary

It is always fashionable to make use of good vocabulary while in conversation with others. The idea is to use the most appropriate words possible, staying put from the practise of using fancy words and jargon which often tend to confuse listeners if they are not from a similar professional field or exhibit the same interest as you. This makes for a recipe for a disastrous conversation and one that is likely to go downhill. With the usage of extravagant and unnecessary words in your sentences, you run the danger of being labeled as more of an exhibitionist. Throw in jargon only when you are in the company of like-minded people who share your area of expertise.

Get into the habit of reading newspapers and books so that you know how to make use of the most suitable words in a situation. Reading also gives you the dual benefit of learning to listen as well as understand what is printed on the page in front of you. There is a reason why many parents put their toddlers into the habit of reading; not only does it inculcate the knowledge of words, but also gives one immense information. The latter can be used while making informed discussions among peers and colleagues. No time is too late. Start now and reap the benefits.

Someone with a rich vocabulary can target a wider range of audiences with their oral and written communication. This means that they can work on creating productive relationships with others ensuring their success. A good vocabulary also allows you to understand information coming from varied and seemingly difficult sources. If you do not face any trouble in reading and interpreting high-level textbooks, you are likely to benefit from materials of advanced education and training in comparison to people who can only understand layman terminologies.

Non-Verbal Communication

Enough has been said on the significance of one's body language in a conversation and the role it plays; it plays a huge part in connecting with others and builds stronger, rewarding relationships. It needs to be emphasized that you should always keep in mind the following points:

- Be inclusive of everyone in a room, i.e., maintain eye contact with as many as you can and refrain from standing/sitting with crossed hands and legs while speaking on a one-on-one basis. These rules form part of basic conversation etiquette and reflect one's interests, affection and attraction towards the audience or the listener.
- Maintain a calm voice while talking; raising voice does no good to anyone, let alone any success, if the purpose of the conversation is to influence decision-making.
- Non-verbal messages conveyed through use of body language, like gestures made by hand, has a huge and long-lasting impact on the listener. If you're trying to influence people and hope they look up to you, getting the listener's attention is critical.
- Refrain from standing too close and invading someone's personal space. This tends to make the other person feel uncomfortable. Your physical proximity to a person should be based on your level of comfort and understanding with the person.
- A handshake, a warm hug, or a pat on the head can convey a great deal about our intentions towards the other person. While these may seem inconsequential, the person in question is likely to catch your vibes. So, ensure you are sincere and genuine while making these gestures.

Confidence and Humility Can Go Hand-in-hand

Carrying yourself with confidence is a necessity in today's world. Your qualities are determined on the basis of the confidence you exhibit—be it in a professional set-up or a personal one. Confidence in oneself includes being sure of yourself and your skillset. It, however, should not be such that it undermines any other being. It does not and should not equate to a superiority complex of any kind. A confident person feels prepared for everyday hurdles that life throws at them; most importantly, they believe in themselves and their abilities, and do not belittle those of others.

Many who carry themselves with confidence are often accused of exhibiting over-confidence, which can be dangerously mixed up with arrogance. Not only will it put forth a poor reflection of your personality, but also hamper the quality of your conversations.

To avoid such judgements, one must remember to be humble and polite. This becomes inclusive of being a good listener. It is not possible for even the most confident person to never have their moments of doubt. There would always come a moment when everything would turn green to them. Under such circumstances, do not feel ashamed to seek help—that is where your humility comes in. Your humility lies in your acceptance of the fact that there cannot be everything that you are aware of, or skilled at. There lies no shame in approaching others for advice. It is good to be aware and keep one's ears open while engaging in a conversation, instead of just being the one who talks. Seek feedback from your colleagues and peers on a regular basis to ascertain the areas you need to work upon and improvise.

Give Compliments

Don't be a miser while giving compliments; give them openly. One of the best ways to establish a good rapport with your listener or audience in a conversation is to compliment them.

Be sure to give compliments for any interesting idea or thought brought forward by them in a conversation. Praise them for their creativity, keeping in mind not to go overboard. If someone brings to table a set of novel ideas, inspires you and those around, goes out of their way to solve a problem, be sure to compliment them. This becomes a sign of appreciation from your side for the concerned person. This will inculcate in the listener a sense of camaraderie and motivate them further to put their best foot forward.

In situations where you are communicating with someone at a senior position than you, you may run the danger of being labeled as a sycophant if the compliments are never-ending and uncalled for. Base your compliments on facts, on aspects you genuinely feel about. Remember, a half-hearted compliment and one which is solely based on the purpose of pleasing the others is easy to identify. Keep your words simple so that there is no room for receiving the compliment sarcastically. Throw in adjectives, but consciously. The idea is to lace your compliment with facts and adjectives suitably describing the person in question and their desirable traits.

It is not to be forgotten that compliments also serve as good conversation starters; it is as simple as admiring somebody's attire, marvelling at their array of knowledge or applauding them for their accolades. It can be used to break the ice between two strangers or ones who have met after a long time. A few kind words can do wonders.

Talk About Areas of Common Interest

So, you have met someone for the first time and wish to strike a rapport with them. Have you not been able to break the ice despite showering them with compliments? Try this: ascertain the areas of your common interests. Find what is it that both of you are equally enthusiastic about. This acts as an impetus in carrying forth the conversation with gusto, keeping it alive. Look for a sitcom, a book, or a favourite author which both of you admire and appreciate. A point to be noted here is that this will require some prior research on your behalf and a sense of taking an initiative. Your success at being able to identify areas of common interests may also be preceded by a series of questions or an interactive discussion on the person's interests and likes.

Be observant of all the little details talked about in a conversation—often, there lies your cues for finding the much-needed common interests. Try not to surprise the person with over-enthusiasm at discovering those similarities; you don't want your dear listener to feel overwhelmed. Listen, ask questions, and talk about your experiences regarding those areas of common interests. However, there might come a time when you run out of discussing the same or never had any, to begin with. Should such a situation arise, you can simply ask about what enthuses them—this can range from their hobbies to any recently visited place or a movie watched. If you wish to dig into the likes and dislikes of your listener, why not initiate a conversation about why you invited them for a meeting to a particular café; talk to them about your favourite dish being served there. This will prompt the other person to comment, and with that, the conversation would get going. You would get to discover which dishes your listener is fond of, or which café they frequent in their free time.

The idea is to keep the initial spark of the conversation going—the spark being talked about need not necessarily be while talking about a potential partner, it can be relating to your friends, family and even colleagues.

Pose Questions

Refrain from being a passive listener. Participate wholeheartedly in the conversation. Ask questions about the aspects you are unsure of, ask as many questions that puzzle you. Do not shy away. This will not only clear all your doubts and help in a wholesome understanding of the topic being discussed, but also enhance your interpersonal relationship with the speaker. It would make for an interactive talk, where both the speaker and the listener are equal participants—the ideal scenario. You can also go for open-ended questions which leaves enough room for paving way for an engaging talk.

However, there are certain situations when an overenthusiasm for asking questions comes to be viewed as seeking the limelight. Take the example of a classroom set-up in a school or a college. There is always a student who raises his hand for clarifications pertaining to any subject. He will have questions ready for each topic, for each subject teacher/professor. This person tends to hog the maximum limelight of the class, especially in front of the teacher/professor. However, it may not be taken in stride by his classmates. He runs the chance of being labeled as an attention seeker, which to some extent, might be true. The questions, after all, are never-ending. You don't want to be a nuisance.

Moving to a healthy and constructive example, think of a situation in which you ask questions in a two-way conversation rather than a one-way chat. You have reached an HR interview round at a firm of your liking. The terms and conditions mentioned by HR have, however, left you confused. Under such circumstances, it becomes acceptable to question and get your doubts cleared from HR before signing the offer letter and any important document that follows. You are about to begin your career with this new firm. Thus, here it becomes your right to ask HR any questions pertaining to the conditions of your employment.

In the end, posing questions becomes an art, which has to be scrupulously mastered so that the balance of the conversation between the two parties remains maintained.

But Answer Too

A conversation can be fraught with many questions and thus deserves its answers. While it is considered healthy to pose questions and get one's curiosity appeased, the importance of providing appropriate answers also forms part of good communication skills. In the course of answering one's questions, we rid them of their doubts and thus develop better interpersonal relationships with the concerned person.

Even in a classroom or an office set-up, the format of question-answer session makes way for greater learning experience and better understanding of concepts. It creates an atmosphere of active conversation. Limiting a conversation to a one-sided talk reduces it to a monologue—one which leaves a stellar impact in theatrical performances, but elicits no importance in corporate and educational setup. If you are looking to participate in theatre, you might consider the former, but if you are in either of the two latter groups, you should stay away from a conversation turning into a monologue at all costs.

By answering somebody's questions, you invest your time in them. While it might come across as unbelievable to some, this leaves the person seeking the answer in awe of you. Your action is appreciated.

When did a Frown Ever Work?

Keep a smile on your face when approaching someone or initiating a conversation. It will add to your charm. However, this does not imply that you are expected to imitate Joaquin Phoenix even when you are crumbling from inside.

Keeping a straight face or one with a frown tends to push people away from you. The logic isn't hard to guess: who would approach someone donning a hostile look. It is human psychology at play here. Imagine two people; one approaching you with a pleasant smile and the other with a frown on their face. Who will you be more eager to initiate a conversation with? It is not a puzzling question that seeks a scientific answer.

Ever heard of the common advice given to interviewees: approach the panel with a smile. It not only induces a sense of confidence in you, but also makes other people confident about you, which in some cases, can chart the course of your future conversations and bend them in your favour.

Not only does smiling help reduce the level of stress-enhancing hormones like cortisol, adrenaline and dopamine, it also increases the level of mood-enhancing hormones like endorphins and lowers blood pressure. While it does you a world of good, it also does good to those around you. Whosoever said that people catch your vibe was not wrong! A smile adds to your attractiveness and brings about positivity. It is an energy catcher; we all need good energy flow for a healthy productive conversation.

Regardless of where you go or who you meet in the world, smiling is a sign of happiness understood and appreciated by all. No matter what the language, a smile is something deciphered by everyone, young and old alike. It crosses the barriers of lingual and national diversities.

It's safe to say that smiling a bit never hurt anyone.

Give an Opportunity to Others to Talk Too

Be an efficient listener. Listening does require efficiency, opposed to the popular belief that the ones comparatively quiet and silent in the conversation are passive. Listening is a skill, and everyone ultimately has to learn it, the easy or the hard way. As repeatedly said, while conversing, keep in mind that you alone are not the speaker and the listener. The other party too is an active participant and therefore, has the right of being heard by you and the rest participating in the conversation.

Take the example of a meeting where people from a particular NGO meet up to discuss the plans of a big event. The meeting is likely to consist of members falling under an organizational pyramid; it would commence with the senior-most person bringing to table, the ideas which are to be further deliberated upon. The discussion then reaches a stage where it is safe to be referred to as a conversation; it is now open for further additions and suggestions. It is often noticed that in this round, as a shy or a seemingly introvert person tries to put forth their viewpoint, he or she is likely to be stopped or interrupted by someone.

This is not an uncommon scenario and is most likely to be witnessed in groups, either with friends or colleagues. While this is a common practise, it needs to be immediately done away with for two alarming reasons: firstly, it is inhibiting the quality of the conversation as not everyone is an equal participant and not every idea is getting a mouthpiece. For a conversation to attain good quality, it is important to ensure that all ideas are brought to table and every person is an active participant. Secondly, the listener is not doing his job well and is instead, interrupting the speaker.

One should know when to stop talking. How would you feel if you were to be stopped or cut in by someone as and while you went on talking about something you felt gravely about? Now stand in that person's shoes and assess the situation. The person is going through the same, and that too in real time and space, while your imagined situation was merely hypothetical.

While keeping the spontaneity of a conversation is of great significance and requires work, bringing in much-needed pauses, ensuring every member of the group gets an equal chance, and their active listeners also assume role of great importance.

These are 10 dialogues to get you started. You can use these on the basis of the situation you find yourself in:

i. How have you been?
ii. Which is the most recent film you enjoyed?
iii. Do you want to get some fresh air?
iv. What keeps you busy these days?
v. How are things at work?
vi. Which is your favourite holiday destination?
vii. I hope your family is doing well.

viii. How is the new city treating you?
ix. How are you coping with the pandemic? (This is part of an everyday conversation now, unfortunately.)
x. Which dish do you enjoy the most?

2

WHAT WORKS BEST AT WORK

'Alone we can do so little; together we can do much better'

—Helen Killer

A smooth communication and one which is not cut in at any stage ensures better performance of individuals and teams at workplace. There is always a need of open channels of communication. Regardless of the organizational hierarchy, which is often unavoidable, it must be ensured that everyone in the room has an equal opportunity to speak and express themselves honestly. It should be kept in mind that nobody is attacked emotionally, religiously, or racially under the garb of 'free expression'.

In most cases, a person is operating as part of a larger team in a workplace. This fact should not be forgotten. It should be remembered that one's actions and words alone can bear consequences which might tend to escalate to larger and fiercer state, taking in its ambit everyone, and in worse case scenarios, even the entire company. Think before you speak, take responsibility for your words, and do not utter insignificant things.

While there is no golden rule which would win you the best employee tag at your workplace, you can still aspire to be a good and efficient worker. It is often suggested that one should let their words do the talking. You can try following some of the ways enlisted in this chapter to see for yourself how communication can really have a lasting impact on your professional life. It not only impacts your journey up the pyramid but also of those around you, who can be either hampered or motivated by your communication skills.

Engage Everyone

This point cannot be stressed upon enough. Under no circumstance should you assume that you are the supreme one, and thus deserve to hog all the limelight. Everyone present in a room deserve equal chance at expressing and communicating what they want to, without facing any inhibiting factors.

It becomes the job of each one of us to bring forth a comfortable and convenient environment where everybody can feel safe enough to being forth their ideas without facing the fear of criticism.

A very simple and doable trick can be this: when someone is about to make a presentation in front of a large audience, introduce the person to the audience first with a round of applause. This would help ease the tension and eliminate inhibitions of the person, if any. You can also pick up random names and ask people to join in the conversation or pose questions to them, being very sure that your selection is not coloured by any criteria. Talking of ideas to promote inclusivity, you can go ahead and talk about some of the mistakes you made as an intern while introducing someone at an office welcome party. Be sure to do this very subtly, so that you do not end up hogging the limelight and making it all about yourself. The end goal should be to help the newcomer get out of their shell and participate openly in a conversation.

Having a meeting which is recurring or repetitive in nature, need not mean that it cannot be engaging. Why not try changing the format of the meeting? Change the location, send more specialized invites than the regular ones, tweak the food menu. Allow participants their own time and space to submit their respective reports back to the ones they report to.

Meetings can be interesting when one adds the element of surprise and excitement. The goal should be to eliminate anything that is mundane and does not encourage everyone to participate.

Boost Confidence

Make conscious choice of words when sitting amid people or when leading a conversation. The onus on you to talk responsibly increases when you are in the latter situation. The words you utter, as we have already established, have the power of making or breaking your image. Yours could be words of encouragement or words of discouragement. We have all come across people of both groups in our lives. Each of us wishes, for the people in question, to maybe have had spared a few negative words said. It could be any experience ranging from our school life to professional ones. Maybe it was when the headmaster decided to insult you in front of your peers in the hope of eliciting better performance on the academic front from you, or when a senior colleague decided to belittle you to break your confidence by pinpointing your ability at handling a big project coming your way for the first time. Did it not always hurt to have received the unsought backlash in the form of those discouraging words?

You can now change the narrative for the many you find around you. Tell the young man running out to the conference room that he looks smart and crisp today. A little compliment never hurt anyone; this might end up boosting his confidence for the day. Go ahead and tell your subordinate, who juggles between two jobs, that his time management skills are nothing short of an inspiration.

If words can be used as a weapon, why can they not be used as a weapon of providing comfort and confidence? We should not forget that everyone is undergoing their own share of struggle and we should be able to be a help, if not a nuisance. We can start by accepting someone for what and who they are, trying not to push them towards a change. If you come across an introvert colleague, you do not have to shove them into the limelight hoping that it would do a world of good to their confidence. Though it's the thought that counts, it would rather be an intrusion into their personal space and even hurt their confidence. You should also remind those around you that everyone goes through moments of low confidence, and no one experiences life without at least facing a little self-doubt. It's always healthy to take a step back sometimes and give yourself the much-needed time; identify the areas you need to work on.

Aid in Decision-Making

Unsolicited advices are not welcomed, but if you see someone facing the blues at workplace, at least approach them with an open ear and a shoulder to lean on. It is only after your approach that you would be able to identify what the other person is going through. The matter at hand could often be relating to work or personal life. In such a situation, resist from the urge to let them know that you understand exactly what they are going through. It is you here who needs to understand that no two individuals can have a similar experience, and thus you do cannot understand in totality what they are going through. There are many factors like varying personality types, upbringing and life events that chalk out different reactions and emotions. Often the person just needs a good listener.

It could also be that the person is in dire need of a second opinion in some matter and is not able to come across anyone who would offer him one. Very gently, ask if you can help with the same. Only on getting a green signal should you go ahead with an advice or a suggestion.

If the person is in need of your help, fix up a time when the two of you can meet conveniently and talk over the issue. Giving advice and aiding someone in decision-making is largely based on how well you are able to communicate with them; this calls for the first and foremost tool of conversation—listening. Listen to what grieves them, troubles them. Get an idea of all the factors contributing to their dismay, which at times, might be more than one. While you may not be able to empathize well, you should try to bring forth your ability to sympathize with the person.

When it comes to helping in making decisions, be sure to help them make informed ones. If your colleague is stuck between choosing a promotion at the current firm and taking up a new job with a higher package, ask them that out of the two what have they waited for the longest time now. However, this cannot be the only way to view to assuage the situation and arrive at a decision. Many factors can be at play. It might be possible that the person can be helped with a career counsellor and thus, you should make a suggestion about the same.

There lies no shame in admitting you are not equipped enough to help someone with their troubles if they come forth to you with one. No person is entirely knowledgeable and it is better to give no advice at all than to give an ill-informed one.

Include Solutions in Your Conversations

Often one has fostered a habit of whining and moaning about anything and everything they come across while conversing with others. Do not be this person. This habit will gradually but inevitably rob you of any personal relationships. People will start to avoid you, for you would then be seen as a nuisance. Nobody likes being surrounded by people who constantly talk of the problems in their lives, the issues they have and the troubles they come across. Drop this habit. Reform.

Talk of solutions. Discuss about them. Instead of participating in informal meetings where each colleague is dissing about something or the other, become part of the solution group. If the manager is repeatedly setting unrealistic deadlines for the team, take it up with him; the only practical and productive thing to do is to take up the matter. Constantly berating the manager and cursing him for not setting realistic expectations is not going to do any good to anyone. Discuss about a new and a more realistic deadline with the manager. State your reasons which make you think why the deadlines should be re-evaluated. Back your arguments with numbers and reasoning.

Initiating a conversation about a solution, not stressing on its outcome is a huge positive step in itself. There is where you are at least making an attempt and taking a stand.

Encourage conversations wherein everyone brainstorms for solutions to issues which have been a cause of worry for many.

Call for informal meetings, if need be. Fix a place, fix a date, send invites. Initiate a dialogue where solutions are brought to the table by anyone and everyone aggrieved. The only criteria to allow a person to speak in this group should be that they are able to share their experiences and solutions. Do not forget that solutions do not come from individuals, but rather from experiences. This group will become the most positive forum you would have ever come across because here, one would focus on arriving at a solution and not look into the problem endlessly. This will induce productivity in the long run across all tiers of the organization.

Being a Telltale is Not Good

Maybe we did this as a child. We were innocent and immature to be able to distinguish the right from wrong. But what excuse would you present for being a telltale now? Is it sheer fun or the need to be the morale police that makes you do so? What can possibly be so enticing about being a telltale? It is certainly not earning you a place in anybody's good books.

Will it not be pure embarrassment to be caught hinting as others' secrets and private affairs which they revealed to us by taking us in confidence. Telltales often justify their actions by putting forth that they were simply pinpointing the wrong that someone had done. The only right way to throw light on somebody's wrongdoings is by bringing it to the attention of the concerned authorities and not by talking about it out in the open. You must practise discretion when brought face to face with a situation wherein somebody's actions are uncalled for and needs to be reported.

Let us not turn into a self-righteous version of both the

judiciary and the executive. Turning into one would make us lose our respectable standing amidst our colleagues who confide in us with confidence. We might also run the danger of being ousted from close groups. People, who once took you in confidence, no longer would; what is worse that nobody would risk trusting you again with their secrets and private affairs.

For example, if a colleague tells you about an extra marital affair, he is having, all you can do here is listen. He needs a listener and not somebody who would judge. You indirectly come under the oath of discretion when you hear somebody's testimony. It is not your job to spread the word about his private life as it was you and you alone who was taken into confidence and not others. This becomes part of social etiquette that many people, at times, blatantly violate. The need to spread information from one cubicle to the next without fail is not what you were signed up for at the firm. By now, many should have made enough notes on 'why to stop being a telltale'. The worst that can happen is that you would be forced to live in social exclusion. So, next time you have an urge to poke your nose into others' business and spread a piece of information with which you have no remote relevance, kindly take a step back.

Don't Speak Behind Other's Back

It is not possible to have the same views as everyone, let alone agree with them. If you are a mature professional, you will refrain from speaking behind others' backs and simply go about minding your business. As previously said, this too will put you in the bad books of those working with you. It often gives birth to gossips, rumours and criticism, which otherwise would have found no way to circulate. Not only does it come across as childish, but is equally unethical too. The rumour that you helped circulate one day might develop into something so disastrous that it would be in nobody's power to be able to control it; the person in question might end up suffering terribly for no fault of his own. Who will one put to blame here? It is not one person but each who added their own fuel to the circulating gossip till it became a gigantic flame.

If you have landed in conflict with a colleague and there is an issue that is bothering you, then talk about it with him, instead of going behind his back and spreading hearsay hoping to get back at him.

In corporate setups, people tend to get into the habit of talking behind their seniors' back and partake in gossiping. Not only is such behaviour and conversation counter-productive, it can also be seen as an attempt at character assassination. While it is admissible that becoming embroiled in office politics is a natural process and something that you cannot stay away from despite your best efforts, it can at least be made sure that your active participation and contribution to it remains nil. Why participate in a conversation which is a mere banter with no productive outcome and no positive impact on the mind and soul? People who get into this poor habit often lack the ability to introspect and are the ones who are quite lonesome in their personal lives.

Talk about Mental Health

Talking about mental health in the corporate world has gained heightened importance. The entire hype created around this is very much justified. Conversations are starting to open up and people are starting to narrate their experiences. This is not only eliminating the inhibitions associated with psychological problems, but also the taboo of discussing about it in front of strangers. Today, every office you come across will have a dedicated HR panel, one that will be working towards ensuring the mental wellbeing of the staff. However, how effective these panels really are is still a question of debate.

One does not have to rely on a formal panel when it comes to maintenance of our mental wellbeing and those of others around you. All it takes to do so is initiate a conversation. If you notice a colleague, who appears to be worn out and visibly in distress, approach the person showing your concern; ask what ails them physically or emotionally.

Leaving behind someone or ignoring someone, despite knowing that they are in need of emotional support is a cowardly thing to do. Now, a selfish person would debate this stating they too have weak moments of their own where they could have used some emotional support to begin with. Here, they should be reminded that even one weak chord can bring down the performance level of the entire group. It thus becomes vital to ensure that every colleague is in a frame of mind where they are able to deliver their best, and not just something average; this is possible by ensuring that they have a healthy environment wherein inter-personal and intra-personal conflicts can be spoken about without the fear of any judgment or criticism.

Who does not run after improved job performance and productivity—you, your boss, your manager, all of them? These are the factors determining your bonus, your appraisals and most importantly, your promotions. For example, imagine that around the time of your performance review during your probationary period, you end up getting down with a high fever which renders you bed-ridden for a week's time. What would you do? Working is not an option; you can barely get up from the bed to go to the bathroom. Under such circumstances, won't you have someone take care of you so that you get well soon and jump back to work hale and hearty putting your best foot forward to compensate for the loss made in the past one week? What stops you then, from approaching another person to seek assistance in getting better, when you are experiencing psychological troubles? For many, acceptance of the fact that they are troubled by some psychological issue, in itself is the first big step.

It is only after helping yourself will you be able to help someone in acute need.

Stay Respectful

Respect those working with you and those around you. Make it evident through your words and action. There might be moments when you feel impassioned by certain thoughts and ideas which are not in coherence with those of others. These thoughts and ideas can be about anything ranging from politics, current events, or a management decision. Practise controlling your emotion and your speech under such circumstances. You are very likely to say things in the heat of the moment which you will come to regret later. Eliminate name-calling, belittling, stereotyping from your words—anything that can possibly hurt the one hearing those words. There is no need to make a conversation heated and personal for it will only add to its chances of turning ugly. Such conversations cannot be fruitful for anybody, let alone a group in a professional set-up.

Stay put from conversations that target a race or ethnicity; do not use racial or ethnic slurs, no matter how informal the group. Many organizations, upon joining, will run you through documents specifying the kind of communication errors you are expected to stay from and would be held guilty for. It has transcended from occupying only the social arena; it now occupies the professional one too. Should you or anyone you know engage in conversation cornering a person based on their race, colour, caste, or religion, you can be heavily penalized for the same. Respect all diversities.

One more way to pay respect to someone in a communication is by keeping an open ear and by being an active listener. This should not and need not follow any criteria; the person can be a junior or a senior to you. The moment you allow someone to talk without interruption you give them your time; this is a manner well-received and appreciated by everyone. Give the other person enough time to explain their ideas without barging in-between. It is the minimum you can do in a conversation at a workplace. The desire to show respect to someone while having a conversation should not be based on your need to flatter them or gain a favourable outcome. Simply do so as a courtesy.

Respect is a two-way process. Expect it in return only after you accord the same respect to that person; else it is just a superiority complex at play.

Your Words are Powerful

Know that your words have consequences—good and bad. The kind of conversation you engage in and the kind of people you engage in those conversations with have an impact that extends beyond the present moment. For example, you are standing in the smoking room and you hear a colleague targeting somebody's character in a conversation. The worst thing you can do here is to participate in that conversation for that can mean the violation of company's norms. These will land you in a legal trouble and strain your associations with the higher-ups in the firm. Words can have negative as well as positive consequences.

Take another example, consider talking to a trainee at the firm you work in. It is her first day and she seems visibly stressed and unnerved. In such a situation, you can engage her in a conversation about the eateries around the office and the plethora of cuisine options they serve. Not only is it an ice-breaker, it will also change the person's current state of mind. Your remarks may not have been groundbreaking, but they did result in a positive outcome. That can be a small yet effective method to make a change with your words.

Words have more to them than their literal meaning; they take on colour depending on how they are used and presented in a conversation. Coupled with distinct body languages, the same word can carry different meanings for different listeners. One's culture or the culture they currently live in, also shapes the way their words are taken and decoded. Words that might be widely acceptable in a particular country may be taken for a rude behaviour in another. So, be cautious of your words and where you use them.

Small Talk Is Okay

The spouse, the kids, the weather, the lunch—these make for excellent topics when we are scrounging for something to start a conversation over with a person we have just met. Even a possibility of small talk leaves many of us gasping for air. It makes many of us feel nervous, claustrophobic and highly cautious of everyone around us. While some consider small talk to be shallow, many call it the opposite of a meaningful conversation.

Fortunately, these are only assumptions.

Small talk, in fact, can be quite fruitful if put to use tactically. To some, this seems an art they long to master. We often come across people laughing cheerfully in a roomful of people, despite the fact that they have met for the first time. The methods of initiating a small talk should not be lost on you, should you find yourself in a situation where you need to do so. Remember, it is not the end of the world. It is not possible for anyone to judge you merely on the basis of the first conversation you ever have with them. Imagine coming across a famous chef in a restro-bar with whom you wish to strike a conversation. The spouse, the kids, the weather, the lunch may not be such good conversation starters in this case. Simply, go and introduce yourself and express your thrill at being able to meet the chef. Say what you mean. By doing so, you will break the chain of negative thoughts in your head, and overcome all apprehensions; what will flow will be a natural course of talks between the two of you. Similarly, while hoping to start a conversation with your manager or a senior colleague, you may find a common ground for discussion first and then pick up the conversation from there.

It will be realized that what is labeled is 'small talk' is nothing but a calculated talk with the hope of taking it to a particular conclusion. It is definitely not rocket science, or anything to be feared.

These are 10 ways to help you initiate a conversation with your colleagues.

i. How has that project been coming along?
ii. Is there any assistance you need?
iii. You look quite bogged down. Why don't we take a

walk? (We all wish we had someone who would rescue us so.)
iv. I see you have read the *Da Vinci Code*? Have you gone ahead with any of the other titles by the author? (The names are purely for the purpose of giving an example. It is not very uncommon to spot a book or two on somebody's work table.)
v. Do you mind giving me some suggestions, please?
vi. Can I please know about the progress of your last project?
vii. What are your weekend plans?
viii. Do you need me to call you a cab?
ix. Do you need an extension for the project (This one is for the managers out there; this is not as bizarre as you think it to be.)
x. I hope your new project goes well. Do let me know in case you need any guidance.

3

LOWERING TEMPER

*'When angry, count to ten before you speak;
if very angry, count to hundred.'*

—Thomas Jefferson

There are *not* many instances in popular account where anger brought about a positive turn in a conversation. You may beg to differ, but let us allow the majority of the readers to lead with the opposite belief.

When not controlled, anger can cause damage that is beyond repair. It is only natural to fall into a situation where one finds them upset and overwhelmed to the extent that it comes out in the form of hostility and displeasure towards something or someone. It is often expressed in the form of yelling, wailing, or even shutting down completely. Every person you come across will have a different way of communicating their anger to you.

While you are experiencing an array of emotions being angry—there is agony, frustration, irritability, resentment—it should not be forgotten who the person standing in front of you is.

It is often suggested that one should not take to heart the words uttered by another in moment of anger. This, however, becomes difficult to follow and understand when the other is your spouse, parent, or a dear friend. On one hand, we exhibit the lack of understanding of how to swallow the harsh words thrown at us, and on the other hand, we also find it tough to refrain ourselves from being the ones doing so. We are both—the receiver and the one perpetrating it. The least we can do is eliminate the possibilities where we end up being the latter. While the mood or situations the other person finds themselves in is entirely beyond our control, what we can definitely control is our temper. This term—though should not be—is often used synonymously with anger. While anger is a feeling of displeasure, having a temper is a tendency of being angry easily. In the chapter, we will mostly stick to the usage of the term 'anger' for easier understanding and keeping confusion at bay.

Note: It is also widely known that high levels of anger add to the risk of coronary heart disease.

Count to 10

We can start with Jefferson's suggestion about counting to 10 if angry before speaking, and to 100 if very angry. Our words, as repeated time and again, have a huge impact on the one at the receiving end. That impact only gets multiplied when the situation involves a heated argument or a discussion. Under the circumstances, one tends to lose control over their language and it becomes more about reflexes taking control. We need to give ourselves enough time for the anger to subside before anything is said in the heat of the moment. This can be done, as Jefferson says, by counting to 10 slowly. Do not forget to do some deep breathing side by side with every count.

Every time, you feel your temper touching the roof, start with the counting. Some would even suggest doing an opposite count for a better calming effect. Choose what works best for you. Ten necessarily might not be your magic number. But it sure will help you diminish the damage that could have been caused had you gone ahead with your immediate reaction in your weak moment. After taking some time off, we are better equipped to respond to the situation, rather than react. It gives us time to analyse what went wrong in the first place and what can be done as a solution. In those few minutes, the focus changes from engaging in the negative thoughts to finding a probable solution.

Anyone and everyone of us can land in a situation where our emotions get ahead of us. You can be a single parent, a new manager, a teacher, or a cop—anger is an inevitable emotion all of us have faced and have repented later. You need not be hard on yourself if things go out of your control and you end up being hurtful for the first time. However, if things have started going southward very often for you, it might be time to consider some anger management. For all you know, you might be in immediate need of a break.

Take a Quick Walk

You need a quick change of environment maybe. As you sense the tension in the atmosphere flaring up, will yourself to leave that place that very moment for some time. To avoid blurting out harsh words that would cause further damage, walk away. This will help you prevent an outburst. It works wonders in saving relationships from landing in perilous situations, often from where there is no coming back. The relationship being talked about, need not be that between spouses, it can be that of a parent-child, siblings, or friends.

Walk out of that room if you know you are about to say something very hurtful. Remember, the person standing in front of you is not your enemy. Even if so, uttering hateful words can never appease anyone's anger, let alone justify it. Another benefit of walking away is that it allows you to watch yourself and gives you the time you need to make an informed decision. We tend to announce important life decisions in bursts of anger, or likewise, negative emotions, which should definitely not be the case.

However, be sure not to make a habit out of this every time you face a difficult situation or one where you need to confront the other. It might be taken as an escapist tendency. If you are stuck in a recurring situation that has become a matter of annoyance for you for quite some time, it is time for some re-evaluation. Switching rooms or taking a quick walk is perhaps not a solution for you anymore. The other person may take it to be as a form of punishment enforced on them, which is not the case, for all you have been trying to do is calm down yourself and watch your words. Try talking to the person when things get calmer and under control.

Identify Possible Solutions

Think of all possible solutions to a situation; range them from the most idealistic to the most doable. List them down. Ponder over them.

Lashing out at someone in anger might seem to be an easy way out in the moment but it will not amount to much productivity; in some cases, the productivity might be next to nil. Rather sit and mediate about what all can be done to assuage the harm caused so far. The first step should be to get to the root of the problem.

Taking care of the matter superficially will not do you, or those around you, any good any more. Invest the time to eliminate from the roots whatever it is that is troubling you. It can be anything from a friend's repetitive unintentional offensive behaviour towards you or a colleague's lack of cooperation in projects you are supposed to work together for. You can deal with such issues differently depending on the severity of the situation and how far you have been able to tackle it. For example, you might consider talking to your friend about their problematic behaviour. However, it might become useless to do so after one point and the only possible remedy you are left with is to walk away from that relationship. Let's take another example, you can call out your colleague on a one-on-one basis for their lack of cooperation. If that fails, try assigning to them their cut of the work that needs to be done and mention what you will be working on side by side. As your third option, approach your manager asking for a replacement in the project to be able to submit it on time.

Every situation comes with a solution. We just need the right frame of mind to be able to arrive at one.

Don't Hold Grudges

We come across experiences in life that leave us hurting for a long time. The process to heal and overcome that becomes tougher when the person in question is a loved one and someone we trusted with all our heart. Most of us under such circumstances end up being resentful towards that person, which unknowingly hampers our personal growth and development in life.

Holding grudges against people who seem to anger you will only impact your mental health in the long run. You will be giving fodder to that growing frustration and negativity in your mind. What good will it do? Release those emotions you have kept bottled up for so long. Cry, yell, lament, acknowledge and let go of that emotion which has been festering inside you like an untreated wound for quite some time now.

For your peace of mind, it becomes imperative to grow out of the emotions that are holding us back in life, preventing us from moving forward. It needs to be understood that holding a grudge also means holding on to past events and recalling them time and again. It will add to your anger and bitterness which can be likely to manifest in the current relationships and even the ones yet to come in your life. You end up becoming so entangled into the wrong, into the past, that the present loses its significance to you—you forget to enjoy the present moment. Feelings of depression and anxiety overwhelm you impacting your overall wellbeing in all aspects of life. When you stick to a grudge, you're giving the person who caused you hurt to continue having an unhindered presence in your life. By giving them space constantly in your thoughts, you are giving them the agency to control your emotions and bring back those moments which leave you angry and frustrated.

Realize the power you possess—you hold the power to steer your life in the direction you choose, you hold the power to invest emotions in situations wisely and adequately. Eliminate the odds from your life. Start living in the present once again. You need to float to the shore to see the violent waves are far behind now.

Forgive and Forget

With letting go of a grudge, you also have to learn to forgive and forget. When it comes to getting over your anger, start doing so by being honest with yourself. Forgiving and forgetting should not be considered equivalent to saying that the offence or hurt caused was justified in any sense. What is done cannot be undone and neither can it be changed for the better. All that lies ahead is acceptance or denial. Heading with the former will be a healthier choice for you. Once you have accepted the status quo, you should push yourself to accept the fact that no matter how apologetic the person is or no matter how ungrateful they are, the past will not be changed and hence forgive; forgive not for them, forgive for yourself. You deserve to welcome new things in life and that cannot be done by staying stuck in the past. Forgiveness is beneficial for your relationship with your partner, your loved ones and your family.

Next step is to forget. You will have to put in the efforts of deleting the memories that cause you hurt and complicate your relationships. While it is easier said than done, at least take a step ahead in that direction. No battles are won overnight. So, we shall proceed with baby steps hoping for the best.

Make space for new memories. Why fill your mind with the residuals of yesterday that serve no purpose and only make you morose every time you recall them? You owe this to your mental wellbeing—do not be dictated by the incidents of the past. They are bound to only add to your frustration. So, forget the time when your parents did not acknowledge your improving grades in science class, forget the time when your best friend did not attend to your calls when you needed them in grief, forget the time when your neighbour thought it was okay to bring up your child's late developmental stages at a party and discuss about it, forget about the time when your favourite teacher punished you for a mistake someone else had made. Move ahead. Anger will not help your cause. Maybe you already do realize that by now, and only need someone to utter it for you.

Change the Perspective

You have been trying to let go of that anger for the longest time you can remember. There is nothing you have not tried to forgive and forget the person who caused you grief and agony in any way. Perhaps, you have been thinking about the entire situation from one point of view. Why not try changing that?

Maybe it is time for you to make efforts to stand in the shoes of the other and look at the situation from their lens, to understand what the situation means to them and how they have been viewing it all along. Doing so might offer you a solution, one that your anger and pent-up emotions had made difficult to look for. As and when you become open to new possibilities of looking at the same situation in different ways, starting with looking it at how that person views it, you will get an understanding of how multidimensional things can be. There is no one way to deal with a situation; the seemingly one way comes in our consciousness following a set number of factors like our morality, upbringing and sense of right and wrong imbibed in us since childhood.

These three factors can be subjective and wary from one family to another. Thus, why do you expect people to have the same viewpoint as yours. It is not always possible and cannot be. Once you accept that there can be more tangents in a situation than yours and yours alone, you begin to get more open to the idea of the other person being right to. This—a simple understanding of the importance of changing perspective—helps to control the raging anger.

For example, you are upset about your mother not being able to make it to your son's first birthday party celebrations. This seems to have created a social distance of sorts between the two of you, with you obviously upset over the fact that she missed the celebrations. Did you try talking to her about why she couldn't make it to the party. There must be a legitimate reason that kept her away from your child's special day. Try standing in her shoes and think why on earth would your mother skip your child's first birthday party knowing how much it means to you. There could be n number of reasons for why she couldn't attend the celebrations. The solution here is to take an initiative and talk to her about it. Do so with an open mind. You will get your reasons and you will form a complex understanding of perspectives which are not always linear.

Think About Them

We are only human. Erring is natural. Isn't everyone forgiven for one mistake at least? Think about the person in front of you and your relationship with them. Is it worthy enough to give up everything you two built together since childhood, or your teen years or your college days, on the basis of one ugly disagreement you have landed in? Think about the importance this person holds in your life and how far you have come along crossing hurdles, big and small, together. Do keep in mind relationships, of any kind, are hard to be formed and easier to be broken; a few unkind words, dismissal of the other's feelings and assertion of yours on the same time can be quite damaging.

Think of all the moments you spent with the person, the kind of joys and sorrows you have seen in life with that person by your side. Are you willing to let go of those memories because of a single incident? The answer here can vary deeply from person to person depending on one's past experience and what they are currently undergoing. If someone has had an abusive father, the person then has no happy thoughts to refer to of his relationship with the father. Under such circumstances, he is likely to sever his link with him. The feelings of anger or hurt might never go away regarding that person, it would rather act as an impetus each time you recall him. Breaking off certain ties, though the hardest decision of your life, can be more important than we realize them to be.

However, imagine a partner who lied to you for the first time and got caught. It definitely infuriates you and heated arguments have already been exchanged. However, would sitting on the issue forever and holding a grudge against them be reasonable? Why not question them about the need to lie in the first place. They sure would be having an explanation to offer. Again, try understanding their perspective and what forced or motivated them to lie—something they usually refrain from.

It is a simple question you need to ask yourself: do you want that person to be a part of your tomorrow? If the answer is yes, then you know what is to be done. You then need to arrive at a conclusion which is acceptable to the both of you, knowing that certain level of compromises should be mutual and not expected solely out of one person. If you consider the person more significant than the issue at hand, then the best thing to do here will be to reconcile and let go of that anger.

Let Them Know

Does your anger go through the roof every time you see that person? Do they remind you of something that you just want to forget? Is it about that time when your colleague touched you inappropriately at an office party; is it about the time when your mother thrashed you for a mistake your older sibling had committed; or is it about the time when your father thought it was for the best to stay away from your mother on Christmas eve and you saw her weeping the next morning?

There is always certain amount of pain and agony we carry deep inside our hearts hoping they never come to the shore else they would create a havoc and destroy everything in its wake. It is not for long that we can dwell in peace with these suppressed emotions. The anger you have been feeling for all this time needs an outlet; a feisty speech battered with all your emotions, most importantly, your anger, might do you some good.

Write everything down, leave out nothing. Sit with them and say what you must. Ask a friend or family member to accompany you when you confront the person. Seeking support and backing out is no act of cowardice. Once face to face, tell them about what is it that has been hurting you for so long and how can it be recuperated. Tell them the day, remind them of the words they uttered or never did. Be specific. This is your moment to rid yourself of the past emotions that your mind has been centring around. Empty your heart in front of that person, for it has carried enough burdens now. It is only right that they should be aware of the turmoil that has been caused by their words and actions. No matter how many days, weeks, months, or years may have passed, some conflicts fester if they remain unattended. It should thus be taken care of with a proper closure.

Arrive at a conclusion and close the chapter for good.

You Cannot Be Enough at Times

Know that it is totally okay to not be able to be enough for someone. People are bound to find mistakes in your personality. Not every two people who meet are suited to one another; there are numerous differences in temperament, upbringing and viewpoint.

There are some easy and obvious ways to know for sure when someone feels you are not enough for them—they are not there to support you emotionally, they have stopped making efforts to be on the same side of things with you, they avoid conversations with you, let alone confrontation, they would constantly try to change certain aspects of you. They will demand of you to become a version of yourself that you may not be even able to identify later. Changing yourself for someone who will always be on a lookout for ways to change you even more is never a wise step to start with.

Suddenly, you seem to be becoming non-existent for the person. They have already decided deep within that you are just not enough. However, each situation calls for an analysis and closure. Be sure to initiate a conversation, whether it is to their liking or not. You owe this conversation to yourself.

The good news in face of such adversity is that you are enough for yourself and the power to uplift you lies within you. So, even if someone tries to demean or abandon you, know your self-worth. Walk away. Some people will never be satisfied with what you do or say. All they remind you is of your inefficiencies and limitations. Walk away from such toxicity. It can be coming from anyone.

You need to identify the person for whom you are never enough and ask yourself whether putting yourself through so much is even remotely justified for a person who does not care enough about your thoughts, ideas and perception of things. People at times set unrealistic expectations from the other without realizing the kind of pressure they are putting them into. Exhausting your emotions, which in turn, affects your physical and mental wellbeing, will only deteriorate your condition.

Change the Topic

Many would agree, when being said, that this stage might come early for many of you and in fact should. It is after all an amicable way of steering clear of what unnerves you. You are well aware of your trigger points and what irks you. You have an understanding of what angers you and what calms you down.

For example, you are in a room full of family members when one uncle decides to crack a sexist joke at the expense of another member. Though you have always stood your ground and debated under such conditions, doing so might not seem a possibility in a room full of people who are supporting and cheering him on. However, the raging anger that develops within you is hard to let go of and even becomes tougher with more family members joining him.

As discussed earlier, you can either choose to walk away from the place or you can change the topic of discussion altogether. If you want to kill two birds with the same stone, introduce such a different topic that it has no parallels to be drawn with the previous one. This would leave everyone in the room unsettled and also put forth your dislike of what was being talked about before. Your displeasure would be conveyed clearly to everyone and anyone good at picking up even the easiest of signs.

Changing the topic of a discussion rapidly and abruptly is often the only way out left for many who are trapped in situations wherein they are meeting extended family members after a long while or are going out for informal office meets. It is safe to assume that there are some people who are simply not aware of the social impropriety of their remarks, that too which are often uncalled for.

Here are 10 ways that can help you out in constructively navigating through your anger:

i. I don't believe we see eye to eye on this.
ii. Maybe what I am suggesting is wrong, what is your take on it?
iii. I beg to differ…
iv. I agree to disagree.
v. I need a ten-minute breather.
vi. Can we please not have this conversation right now?
vii. We need to talk about what happened.
viii. I don't appreciate what you said. It hurt my feelings.
ix. Maybe we need to take some time off to cool off our minds?
x. Let's not make hasty decisions in the heat of the moment.

4

WINNING DIPLOMATIC BATTLES

'Diplomacy is the velvet glove that cloaks the fist of power.'

—Robin Hobb

Diplomacy is an art. It has also become a skill that everyone must learn in today's date. How do you otherwise expect to survive in the toxic competitive world that you are now part of? Diplomacy has become a necessity; be it while talking about two nations or two individuals, some level of diplomacy has to be practised to ensure the smooth functioning of both.

For the world to not be in a constant state of war, we need diplomacy. It is only with the help of diplomacy that peace prevails in certain nations. Handling a dicey affair without arousing hostility is not an art one is simply born with. It lies in the ability of increasing a group's advantage by the maximum possibility, also ensuring that no usage of force is seen or resentment is caused.

However, it is true that it comes easy to some than others. Diplomacy then, as it must be understood, becomes a word game. The one rule that we must adhere to is the selection of words in our conversations—each word should hold significance. Often, the number of opportunities that comes our way to engage in a diplomatic conversation is less. We can either make the most of it, or lose it completely to the other party. Both chances exist in equal possibilities. Therefore, under such circumstances, the only tool we have in our defence is the words we engage with. Our only chance at striking a favourable deal lays in our ability to present our side of the story in such a manner that it becomes undeniable.

Whoever thought that diplomacy only runs through a network of foreign offices, embassies, legations, consulates, or special missions around the world is wrong. We never know when life throws at us a situation which we need to handle tactfully and without running the danger of offending someone. It could be anything, right from a professional crisis to a personal one. Ensuring that the conclusion is in our favour becomes important to all of us. Lacing our words with accurate and just the right amount of information forms the basis of winning diplomatic battles. But that is not all. It includes not only getting across your idea, your part of the deal, but also ensuring that it is accepted without causing conflict, stress and offence.

The following points talk in detail about some of the ways in which you can win your diplomatic battles.

Keep in Contact with Everyone

While traversing through different stages of life, we tend to miss out on various people we once knew well. This is something we need to rectify and stop doing. It never hurts to stay in touch with people. Though it can sound taxing and like a lot of work, it sure has its own benefits.

No matter how selfish it may sound, keeping in contact with people can prove to be beneficial to you, even when you least expect it to. We unknowingly find ourselves in situations we never thought we would be in. Such situations might call for gathering pieces of information and details that we single-handedly might not be able to. This is when that high school friend or an old colleague from your previous firm suddenly pops up in your head. They might be able to help you somehow with the situation. However, it is only possible one way. You cannot and should not go on initiating a conversation expressing the need for their help years after you severed all connections with them or made no effort to stay in touch. Maintaining relationships takes efforts and you cannot escape the hard work when hoping to stay in touch with everyone.

Once in a while inquire about how they have been doing, talk about their family, any hardships if being faced. Be there for them when they need you to. There is no complicated mantra to stay in each other's lives if you intend to do so. For some, having a lot of friends works, for others, simply having many acquaintances does. Only the presence of a fluid conversation between the two parties can facilitate you to approach them for help of any kind. This is, however, not to be mistaken with selfish relationships that only exist to enjoy its fruits.

Reveal Only What You Must

Another key element of maintaining a diplomatic conversation is that you should only reveal pieces of information that are absolutely necessary to be revealed. Putting forth all your cards in front of the one with whom you are striking a diplomatic conversation might amount to foolhardy.

Decide beforehand, what is it that you must bring to the

table while discussing a topic with the concerned person. Make a mental note of the points that you must not leak, not even remotely discuss. Certain pieces of information carry with them the ability to make or break a deal. People have the ability to twist and use whatever information they get their hands on, to their benefit. Under such circumstances, it becomes even more imperative to utter only what *must* be said.

For example, it might be the appraisal season at your work. While you are looking forward to a hefty increment, you are also applying for other jobs for a salary increment. A colleague of yours already have had their appraisal and you wish to inquire about it. Now, while doing so, you must stay wary of not disclosing the fact that you are applying to other jobs hoping for an increment at the present one. You may run the risk of being exposed by that colleague. This will put in jeopardy, your chances at getting an increment at your present job.

At times, we tend to expose ourselves and divulge too much information while striking a conversation. It should be realized that this trait of ours can go against us. As for the above example, we need not talk about our secondary plans that we have been making. Simply, inquire about what you need to know, separating it from any sensitive information you might be having about the same. Convey to the person what impacts them directly, else, prefer to stay mum.

Honesty Might Not Be the Best Policy

In continuity of the last remark, refrain from being cent per cent honest with the person in front of you while engaging in a diplomatic conversation. You are bound by no moral righteousness to present everything you know, all the knowledge you harbour. When you intend to make a difference with whatever you are sharing, you have to consciously make the effort to not speak the truth. For favourable outcome, you need to create a conversation such that the maximum results are achieved by exposing least information from your side.

You must know that what is true or seemingly harmless for you need not be so for the other party too; they might view it negatively or as a potential threat.

In case of confusion regarding what must be revealed and what must not, approach a senior person, be it in your school, college, office, or home. Seek counsel, if you must. Decide on what is appropriate enough information to be shared with the other person.

Another example could be an interview round with your dream company. It is rare that a completely honest answer will win you the favour of the interviewers and the HR. Very often, people prepare answers for probable questions that can come up in interviews beforehand. Even here, being a 100 per cent truthful can have adverse impact on you. If you left your previous company following a tiff with your boss, you cannot state the same at the reason while applying for new jobs. It would create a poor impression of you among those interviewing you. For worse, they might take you as one who picks up fights at workplace or is unprofessional. This can be one of the best real-life examples where the need for diplomacy kicks in; this can be done by masking your real thoughts with more acceptable ones. You can simply state the need for better exposure and salary structure as your prime reasons for quitting your former job. While it is safe to hold back 100 per cent truth in certain situations, it is not recommended to lie in every other situation. You do not want to end up in a web of your lies with nobody knowing anything real about you. As complicated as it may sound, diplomacy is truly an art.

Avoid Pointing Fingers

Stay put from pointing fingers at others. Accept your mistakes, no matter how big or small. You are engaging in a diplomatic talk to arrive at a solution amicably without offending or upsetting anyone. The goal is to arrive at a favourable outcome without causing any damage to the present or future ties with the opposite party.

By pointing fingers or accusing others for something that has affected both parties negatively, you will only move away from your goal further. There should be no escalation of tensions from the two sides at any cost. Anger, more animosity and venting of frustration at the site would only add to the drama. You have not come for a debate but to arrive at a solution to a problem that has already consumed much of your time. A constructive discussion should be the end goal of both the parties; it should not be a confrontation of any kind. The conversation, under such circumstances, need to be delicately handled because the displacement of any latent anger can lead to the entire action and efforts becoming futile. Both the parties will then reach back to square one. It will once again be a long journey then.

While pointing fingers at the other party, one also tends to indulge in mudslinging. This is yet another practise that needs to stop. Stop being fixated on finding faults with each other, for that would serve absolutely no purpose but will give birth to more negativity. Places where blame culture is prevalent are also bound to have scapegoats—individuals who end up being blamed for the action of others and bearing the brunt of it all.

Any individual can become a victim of this. Hence, the practise of pointing fingers at others should be entirely discarded in the first place itself.

Exhibit Leadership Skills

To be able to win diplomatic conversations, it is vital that every member of a team is on the same page with the latest developments of the group and at times, also that of the other. This can be done only by ensuring that an appropriate person is holding the reins of the team so that no member goes astray. Each member should be informed of what the team is moving ahead with in terms of policies, decisions and development. The front that you present should appear as a united one in all aspects so that that the opposing party does not get any opportunity for finding a weak cord within your group.

You should be able to take charge of teams and duties with minimum interference. Learn to take responsibility for the mistakes of your teammates instead of pointing fingers at them in front of others. How do you expect diplomacy to work if you are not able to manage and salvage situations arising from your own end? At times, we won't even be an appointed leader of a group, but nevertheless should come forward taking the initiative of being one.

In times of need, emerge as the person who would take people out of hopelessness and help them arrive at a solution. Become your own saviour and in doing so, you will automatically lead many out of distress by being their leader. While some people choose to be leaders, others are pushed to be by circumstance.

Think positively and proactively. Say yes to diversity and look at the bigger picture. Identify and analyse what assumes greater importance in larger scope of things and what works best for a larger group of people. This will help you make informed decisions and be able to conduct fruitful diplomatic talks in your favour. Work towards achieving the goal and stay put from anything that bothers you or acts as a deterrent.

Know Communication Style of the Other

Everybody has their own communication style. Some are passive, some are aggressive, some are passive-aggressive and some are assertive. If you talk to an aggressive person in a passive tone, the conversation might as well be viewed as null and void. The person who readily accepts what others are doing or proposing without much of their own active response or resistance cannot be considered fit to participate in diplomatic conversations. Same goes for the two other types. We need to identify these communication traits in the people we meet, and even try to adopt the same while attempting to strike a conversation with them. This can be done by asking questions, being observant and listening carefully. This can be extremely useful while engaging in diplomatic talks as you will stand a greater chance at success by dealing with the opposing party the way they deal with others. Similar communication traits are likely to give birth to fruitful talks.

Paying close attention to how one communicates can reveal many facets of their personality. We would get a better understanding about the usage of specific terms used by the person or the inner group to which they belong; those words might come across as jargon to us first. Adopting and quickly adapting to the way one communicates can be to one's advantage. We too then can talk to them in the manner they are used to and known for. This would eliminate further possibility of us being treated as aliens and we would get a chance to be part of the in-group.

Understanding somebody's communication style would obviously help us form better relationship with that person.

Pursuing diplomatic conversations becomes easy when you have insight into the way the opposing party communicates. You will then have an upper hand in communicating with them the way they know and are used to. There would be no room for clashes.

Never Give Strong Reactions

Avoid giving strong reactions to the other person/party you are engaging in diplomatic dialogues with. Whatever has been achieved and built till date can go crumbling down with the heightened use of speeches. Stay put from hyperbolic references and remarks, stay put from any reaction which can infuriate the other party and push your agendas into jeopardy.

Giving strong reactions can also have an impact on the future of your relationship and your future conversations. It can cause long-term damage and distort the course of development you were on in relation to the topic. Always remind yourself of the reason why you are interacting with the person and why the conversation is being held. The task needs to be done amicably and not by resorting to any means of violence. This will help you control your impulsive reaction to the situation. There should always be a difference between your real emotions that you wish to express and the ones you end up emoting; in case of any lapse, the opposition or simply the other person can rise to the occasion and end up beating you.

Reserve your real emotions and reactions only for those who have stood by your side through thick and thin and seen the wheel of time turn with you. Not everybody can be trusted and the ones you do must be selected very wisely. They can help you succeed or give you away. It may be sounding like a gamble to many, for gamble it is.

Be Tactful

Never forget that while holding a diplomatic conversation or trying to initiate one, you should always be tactful. This can include being considerate of others' feelings, saying the correct things to salvage a situation, discretion and self-awareness. Being tactful does not come naturally to people; you can only learn it through time, experience and efforts. You can also learn by observing others who are known for their tactfulness.

Often politicians are the best example of ones representing tactful behaviour. This becomes even more evident around the election season when the time comes to garner vote and support by hook or by crook. They will gather the people living around and attend to their woes and complaints 'considerately'. They tread with the awareness of the fact that it is in the hands of the voters where the power lies. Thus, they know how to preserve and get the most of the voter-representative relationship. They are also aware of their limitations and how the same can be used to the advantage of the opposing party. So, here comes self-awareness—another important aspect of being tactful.

Your body language should be in coherence with the ideas you choose to discuss and the stand you take on a particular situation. There should not be any room for its lack for that will again give an upper hand to the other party. They might dig into that incoherence and present it as a weakness of your group; it can also be considered as a lack of confidence when what you communicate non-verbally is not going with your presented words and ideas. Making up for a strong argument would therefore become tougher.

Be Polite

The key component of a diplomatic conversation is the decorum and politeness it calls for. Shouting and yelling will not help you get your point across. It will only complicate the matters further, and you have assembled on a common platform as your opposition to achieve the exact opposite. A solution can only be arrived at by keeping in mind that one must respect and be polite towards the other party, no matter what their goals and aspirations. The decorum of the conversation must be maintained so that the issue at hand does not get escalated for the worst.

The meeting of military leaders of various nations for de-escalation in certain war-prone areas is the perfect example of what can happen if decorum is not taken care of. It has often been observed that when one country becomes totally submissive of the requests of the other, it ends up infuriating the latter. In the end, the talks end up becoming a failed exercise at attaining peace and de-escalation.

Though there are bound to come many moments when you would be tempted to resort to name-calling and make use of language not suitable to be heard at such a forum, caution is what you must exercise. Do not thrive under a superiority complex thinking that the ideas and views presented by you and your team are alone capable of being announced as the best. On the contrary, objections will be raised, fingers will be pointed and mudslinging would take place. There is no escape from that. However, even under the direst of circumstances, one should remember to not lose their calm and composure. The basic etiquette of a diplomatic conversation should be maintained at all costs. It is with a certain objective in mind that the two parties have met, and the emphasis should be laid on striving towards the same. Do not make personal remarks or attack somebody's limitations that can't be helped with; if done so, you would be stooping down to newer lows.

Being polite is an underrated term as is very often mistaken for simplicity and foolishness. Avoid usage of negative terms or anything that is likely to sabotage your conversation.

Be Assertive

Stick to your point. Be assertive. It is the opposition's task to dissuade you from pursuing your goal. Your task is not only to reach your goal, but also convince the other party of why your points stand true and valid. Be prepared with proper justification of the same. Your side of the arguments should not seem weakened at any point. This can be done without anger flaring up from both sides and being disrespectful of the others' viewpoints. All you need to do here is to stand your ground and remember what is it that you strive for. Be very clear and open about what you want while communicating with the other party. Be straightforward about it, such that there is no room for miscommunication and maximum benefits are attained through the discussions.

No matter what your feelings are regarding the topics brought to the table, be clear about your feelings keeping in mind that no sentiments are hurt and nobody is offended. Being assertive goes hand-in-hand with being polite. You cannot be one without being the other.

Another part of being assertive is the maintenance of your body posture. Sit upright without any visible signs of conflict or animosity like folded hands across the chest and crossed legs. Apart from that, do not forget to do your homework before arriving for the conversation or the discussion. If necessary, take out considerable time for it. It will help you enlist your discussion points precisely. Lastly, being assertive should not mean, at any cost, that you lose your calm and cool. You have to win a diplomatic conversation on the merits of the value addition that you bring to the table and not on the basis of accusations thrown at the other group.

Tap into Your Powerhouse

Always be aware of your strengths and weaknesses. Make sure every team member is aware of these. These can be seen as the powerhouse of your bargaining skills and negotiations. Make all possible efforts to shield or subvert your remaining weakness into strengths so that they are not used against you. While looking forward to a favourable outcome, you need to know that you cannot have your way every time. Know your worth and what is it you are negotiating for. You and your teammates should have a full understanding of what you are aiming for.

Various facets of the topic to be discussed or being discussed might be novel and unprecedented. This can be put to good use while negotiation. So, you need to bring this fact to the table such that it works in your favour.

And this you should be able to digest. There needs to be

an acceptance of this fact. The idea is to embrace flexibility so that you are able to move across from one point of view to its better version without wasting much time. Being rigid will stop your growth and also inhibit the growth of your teammates.

The smartness lies in evolving with times. What is redundant and seems to bring about no productivity should be abandoned. Learn to go with the flow of things. You do not know who the next workable idea might be coming from. It could be from any of your oldest colleagues or a newly hired trainee. Always keep your mind and ears open. Always stay receptive.

You should come prepared with a back-up strategy, so that in the case of the failure of one, another can be implemented and put to use. This helps you to stay on the safer side of things. You should be ready to accept ideas that have more gravity to them. The negotiations are being made for the larger good and not just for your profit alone. It is likely that there are many people who will be affected directly or indirectly by the decision taken.

You can try to keep these 10 examples in mind when you indulge in a diplomatic conversation again.

i. I am not trying to nullify what you said, but... (put forth your point in the argument)
ii. We can go over again what you said. Why don't we start that with my point?
iii. I am offering you the finest deal available, Madam. It's a win-win...
iv. I understand where you are coming from Sir, but...
v. Why don't we discuss the terms and conditions again?
vi. Let us try to re-evaluate the intern and focus on the brighter side of things.

vii. The home-work may be done tomorrow, but then the movie will be deferred too.
viii. We can stick to the original plan, but we need to introduce minor changes.
ix. Why don't we fix up a meeting tomorrow? Today might be tough with me and even you have classes.
x. We will withdraw our troops, but it is required of you to do that first. (Now, do not consider this as a coffee table talk.)

5

PUT YOURSELF IN THEIR SHOES

'I believe empathy is the most essential quality of civilization.'

—Roger Ebert

It is not everybody's cup of tea. But we can at least strive to achieve it. Trying to put yourself in the shoes of others can help you understand their dilemma from their perspective. It opens you to new avenues of understanding. It brings to you the ability to empathize.

Nobody is a born empath; people come across situations in life where they understand the importance of deciphering the other's emotional upheaval. It is only after encountering such situations that one takes the first step towards becoming an empath.

There is a growing need of more people who can empathize in today's time when people suffer from broken relationships and are distant from friends and families. It can depend on multiple factors like the immediate surroundings of the person, their upbringing, the people they grew up with, and the people they are friends with. Several factors work together to determine the empathetic abilities of a person. Being empathetic ranges from being able to listen to what others have to express without giving any judgements about the same; you are there for the person in that moment selflessly. The main idea is to be able to help the other give an outlet to their emotions without the fear of being criticized for the same. Now, that is a quality which is difficult to be found in people today.

Once you are able to understand what somebody has went through emotionally and to what extent, you will also gain an understanding of how to support and help them overcome the same. Though, it can be a time taking process and can vary from one situation to the other.

A conversation with an empath is viewed as therapy by many. Though it might not be a common occurrence to come across one who is empathetic towards your plight, you can play the role for others in need. All you need to possess is the willingness to hear someone out without any bias and listen to them without any pre-conceived notions in mind. Keep your heart open while listening to them as they share their sorrows and agony with you. Remember, that for many, you are probably the last resort in seeking help and they are hanging on to you emotionally, for support and kindness. Be the person you wish you had in your dark times.

Engaging in a conversation as an empath can have its own challenges for you feel strongly about what others are going through. It is due to your ability to gauge their pain that people open up to you quick. There is no manual out there to follow and become an empath. You can go through the following suggestions to be able to try and empathize with someone in need who comes across you. But remember, there is no fixed mantra.

Show Care and Concern

It can be easily deciphered when one is stressed out and is barely hanging by a thread. But what is to be done to help such people? Shower them with care and concern. Let them know that there is someone willing to help them emotionally in case of need. Check on them as frequently as you can.

There is a possibility that they are not surrounded by many who can approach them and ensure they are okay. Be that one person for them to not let them feel alone. Initiate a conversation; talk about what has been bothering them lately. Be genuine in your concern. Slowly and eventually, they will open up to you.

You are not required to go and mark an attendance of yourself on a daily basis to show and prove your care and concern for the person. You can leave behind simple yet touching gestures that will remind them of your presence even when you are not around to do so. For example, you can leave behind some post-it notes on the refrigerator reminding them to have dinner; get their favourite book delivered to them at their doorstep; cook the one dish they savour in every joy and sorrow. Help them live in the present, and remind them that you keep them in your thoughts.

We often commit the mistake of being good to people in the highs of their lives and let them be when they are suffering through the lows. It is the latter which has pushed many to the brink of loneliness and later, suicide. It is often not the absence of people in one's life, but the absence of people we feel close and safe with. Opening one's heart to anyone might pose as a hardship for many and hence, they prefer staying aloof suffering in silence. Many people carrying burden in their heart and mind can be found around—they can be found in your neighbourhood, workplace and college or even among your family members. You just need to be receptive and open to how people around you are faring mentally. Amidst this, don't forget to take good care of yourself too.

Acknowledge Their Emotions

Often people undergoing a shock become dismissive of their emotions. They refrain from acknowledging it, let alone feel it. It is important that sooner or later they come to terms with whatever has happened in their lives and emote themselves well. Holding themselves back infinitely will do them no good; instead, it will further delay their healing process.

Help such people come to terms with their grief. But first, make sure that you are able to be there for them the moment they actually break down and start feeling all those captive emotions in their overwhelming gravity and entirety. Sit them down and help them understand that it is okay and justified to feel so. You must ensure that they know about the legitimacy of their emotions. It is with the help of your acknowledgment that they will come to accept their feelings. Sometimes, one needs another to serve as an impetus in helping us free our pent-up emotions. That again, is completely acceptable. Encourage them to cry, yell, wail, be angry; an emotion kept with a closed lid for too long starts eating you up.

They will take time to open up to you. Once that happens, only then will they start opening up to themselves. These are time taking processes. Do not hurry them into anything, lest they will only end up feeling overwhelmed. Approach them slowly with nothing but the purpose of their healing in your heart. Once you approach them with an open heart, it will be easier for you to understand their grief and what ails them. As they start talking or expressing their emotions even in the least obvious ways, keep your ears open. Be receptive to anything and everything they say. Keep on reminding them that they are doing a great job at being open about their wounds. This will push them out of their cocoon and help them feel accepted; acceptance becomes the biggest asset to them. As an empath, your role is to not coerce them into speaking about their emotions, but be ready to pick up even the faintest of non-verbal communication signs that come your way. That is how they will attempt to converse with you in the beginning. Be quick to pick up those signs. You can form your basis of further conversation with them on the basis of those signs.

Don't Judge

Nobody is a product of their past mistakes and the wrong done to them. Their identity is not to be mixed with what they have experienced till date. They are likely to have been influenced, but should not be seen or understood merely in the light of the incidents which have followed them unfortunately.

Stay put from making any remarks after they share with you any experience of their life. You do not have to be a judge of what they say and what they do. Your purpose is to offer them the comfort and solace that nobody else could. You are there to empathize with them. If you go on judging and criticizing their past decisions and its associated present thoughts, you would become one of the many people who have made them feel targeted in the past.

Do the job of being a good listener. Hear them; watch them unravel their stories after ages of silence and refusal to acknowledge the same. This is the time when they will need a person full of patience to hear them out without any harsh comments, without uttering any ifs and buts. The criterion is simple; you just have to remember that you are there to make feel them secure and not alienated, owing to what they feel or have undergone. Create a safe environment for them by constant assurances that whatever they feel or end up saying will remain between the two of you and that they won't be judged at all on the basis of what they reveal. You should also genuinely believe in these promises and assurances you are giving.

Let this conversation be one sided, with you, being the active listener and the person being the one to talk. Do not expect the floodgates to open in the first go itself. They will not achieve catharsis or anything of the similar effect in one go, and hence, that brings upon you the task of letting them have their time. Assure them that they will be heard whenever they wish to talk. Make yourself approachable to them; leave behind your contact numbers. Tell their families and friends that you can be contacted whenever needed. It is often noted that friends and families who know us too well often pass remarks and comments when we talk about our inner feelings. This leaves us hanging in a state of emotional depravity where we do not know anymore—how to express our feelings without finding ourselves in a vulnerable zone. If lucky, we then come across a person who is simply ready to listen us speak, rant and complain without passing any judgements. That becomes our safe place. The person becomes our safe home.

Encourage to Talk

Read into the fragility of the situation correctly and if you find it to be appropriate, encourage them to talk about what they have been going through. While you should not rush them into speaking, you can at least start with asking certain open-ended questions. A simple example of this could be, 'How have you been feeling lately?' Anything that will help them sit and ponder over the feelings they are being dismissive about lately, can be helpful. The questions asked should be such that the answers cannot be given in a simple yes or a no. Make the questions sound genuine. Don't initiate a conversation they have been dreading while all of you are seated amongst a crowd full of families and friends. It is always better to get them talking on a one-on-one basis. Initiating a conversation about their mental wellbeing with acquaintances around puts the person in a vulnerable situation. Here, we will not have any control over how the situation might turn out to be. You never know who amongst those around would end up passing a hurtful comment when and where. Tread with caution. If you want to get the person talking, approach them when they are by themselves and when they have the time to be emotionally involved in such a conversation. Work on a schedule that suits them and will not end up causing more damage than repair.

If you have a classmate who has started preferring to be by himself and would seldom participate in any class activities, or even eat his lunch by himself, you may try walking up to him. Note his routine and approach him when you find him not doing much. You can invite him over to your table to share your food or you may humbly ask if there is anything you could help them with. It doesn't have to be a big gesture. Making them talk will help them release their pent-up emotions or simply get out of their cocoon. Learn the difference between a person's personality type and a changed behaviour. It would not be uncommon if you mistake an introvert person at a party for someone who is going through a personal trauma. Though the situation can be a possibility, the same can be applicable even to the star of the party who has everyone's attention already. Let us not move ahead with presumptions.

Once you have got the person to talk, you can figure out a solution for them (if the person wants one). If needed, the two of you can sit together and chart out possible course of actions that can be taken to get out of the troubling situation or to let go of the emotion the person has been bounded by. You may rope in professional help if the person is willing to opt for it. To simply get the person to talk should not be the first and the last goal. That is usually the first step to healing and first step of your role as an empath.

Don't Hustle

Having a hurried conversation with a person who is reeling under distress is as good as having no conversation at all. They might be clever enough to catch that you are not genuinely interested in helping them and are perhaps only taking the initiative out of goodwill that you harbour for everyone around. They will not open up to you, let alone give you an opportunity to help them.

Start a conversation when you have the time to invest in the person's affairs and when you can lend them a year without looking at your wristwatch every 10 minutes. You are under no moral obligation to cater to the person's emotional needs, but if you choose to do so, make it your best attempt. There cannot be any shortcuts when you are attempting to share and understand the pain of the other. It is a process that will unfold in its due time and at its own pace. There is not much you can do apart from being there in the moment exhibiting calm and patience.

It should be understood that the one whose pain you are trying to share has not been assigned to you as a project which comes with a deadline. You need to make the person comfortable around yourself and that will take time and efforts. Nobody opens up to a complete stranger or someone they have only known for a while. For this, you will have to make sure that you spend considerable time with the person. Time heals everything and healing takes time.

Silence your phone, stop fidgeting with your car key and refrain from using affirmative words in between the conversation every now and then. Your sole attention should be on the person who has taken great pains to be able to instil their trust in someone and who is attempting to unload their heart and mind of the pain that they have carried for too long. Do not make them feel like they are being taken care of out of mere pity and that they are keeping you away from work and places you'd rather be at.

Silence is Okay

Silence too, forms an important component of a conversation. It gives everyone—introverts and extroverts alike—the time they need to recollect their thoughts. It will give both of you the time to think and analyse what has been said and what needs to be said. Silence can be productive, as opposed to popular belief. You should let go of the habit of being wary of silence or being uncomfortable in a situation which calls for it. Sometimes, all a troubled person needs is the company of others in complete silence. You don't have to fill such moments with words. Do the bare minimum and simply be there in the moment. That's all that is needed of you probably. Nothing less, nothing more.

Silence can also be a way of adding freedom to the bond that you share with the person; this freedom is not dependable on endless consoling, words and counselling. The silence in itself becomes the most powerful tool and aid that can be used to come to their rescue.

Silence becomes a way of communicating to the other that you are there for them emotionally in the moment. It assures them of companionship. It can have a calming effect on the other who, till date, has only heard people talk, chatter, blurt out words to them which seldom amount to anything. Remaining in silence is, however, not to be held synonymous to disengaging from an active conversation.

Once you go silent, it will allow the other person to dig deeper into their troubles. They might not suddenly start talking at lengths, but will try expressing them at intervals. You should, in fact, make the maximum use of non-verbal modes of communication under such a situation. You can still offer them your unconditional support. Stick to the following points:

- Look interested and engaged. Make sure you maintain eye contact with them every time they turn towards you.
- Give affirmations in the form of nods, as and when needed. You don't have to indulge in extensive speeches to let them know that you agree with their viewpoint and understand where they are coming from.
- Give them a gentle pat on their hand. This would show that you support them and will continue doing so. It is a reassuring gesture.
- Give a soft smile. A tender smile to a person who is healing is no less than being told that 'this too shall pass'.

Stop with Those Advices

Your role as an empath entails active listening. There would be minimal difference between you and their next-door person if you start giving advices heedlessly to the ones who are aggrieved or going through a rough patch in life. Had they been in need of advice or suggestions, they would have asked for the same. But such has not been the case.

You find them visibly moved and aloof. A word or two on how to get back to normal will not help their case. No matter how tempting it may be, refrain from giving unsolicited advice. This cannot be stressed upon enough. For all you know, taking suggestions from every third person they come across might be adding to their frustration and taking them further away from any scope of healing. This can cause more harm than imagined and reverse the process of getting better. Suggestions and advice are not what a person needs at times, they just need a selfless company who will be right across them just hearing them talk. If you come to think of it, it can have a therapeutic effect on them. Remember the time when you needed a listener desperately and all you could get was advice and suggestions, coming from left, right and centre?

Maybe what they need is a person who would sit and listen to them rant, cry, complain without passing any remark and suggestion on how to overcome the same. Be that person to them. This is where the art of sitting in silence and still being able to communicate your support comes in. You can also assure them of how you would not leave their side come what may. Help them feel secure and not like an outcast for undergoing emotional turmoil.

Instead of bombarding them with suggestions, what you

should as an empath, do is to ask questions about their wellbeing. Inquire about what they need help with; what is it that they need you to help them with. Be emotionally invested and not just superficially or for the moment. People can sooner or later identify who genuinely means them good and who is there to soothe them just for the time being.

It Is Not About You

As and when they start opening up to you about their woes and troubles, do not interrupt them at any moment with stories of your own experiences. Many commit the mistake of drawing parallels between their own life and that of the other person. This should be avoided at all costs no matter how susceptible you are to falling to its temptation.

You are there to relieve them of their sorrow and not present a lecture on how you overcame yours. If you are in your 50s and have come across a high school kid struggling with ascertaining their future prospects, do not initiate a conversation by telling them how you decided on your career and zeroed down on your passion in life. As an empath, it should be about the other and not about you. You have lived through that phase and there is no need to recapitulate that unless and until the kid asks you questions regarding your own experience. Only if such is the case can you go on talking about your step-by-step evolution.

Every individual is unique and so are their life experiences. Comparing the two will do no good and will only aggravate the anxiety of the person. Let them narrate their story and take a step back, standing in the background. Become a cushion so that they can comfortably fall back on you if they happen to fall and not succeed at telling their story. Be their backbone.

But let them do the tough part—the talking.

Let the person grab the limelight; let them know that they have your attention then and there. Do not cause them to question this in any scenario.

Take the Final Call

You have listened at length, analysed, felt the pain and the agony of the other too well by now. You understand by now, the causes of their ailment, what aggrieves them and how they have struggled to come out of that cocoon. Put these vital bits of information to use. Getting to know the person so closely and understanding their perspective should not go to waste at any cost. A lot of time was invested in helping the person to get out of the shadowy lanes.

Seek a solution on the person's behalf. First, of course, you should take the person in confidence. If they are comfortable and looking for solution, talk to them about what you think will best suit the situation. With their nod, go ahead to seek professional intervention of a counsellor or a psychiatrist, if you must. Often the matter has taken such a turn that it grows out of your control and that of the person; it is here when you will be needing the help of a professional. A childhood mental trauma, loss of a spouse, loss of a child/parent, a life-changing accident—any of these can leave one mentally paralysed and gasping for freedom from the emotional constraints brought about.

Once they open up to you and reach out for help, chart out a probable course of action and share it with them. Your role as empath doesn't come to an end after you are done listening to them talk to their heart's content. Help them emerge as a free person once again. You have, after all, closely seen the pain they carry within. Become the source through which their healing begins.

Help Yourself Too

There is no reason why you should forget yourself in the pursuit of bringing solace to others. Service begins with taking care of the self. You must not forget that. Dealing with conflicts you find yourself in can be emotionally exhausting for you. There is no reason why you would not feel drained. There is the burden of being able to understand what the other is going through and also your own feelings. You have already analysed and studied the problem to a great extent.

It is true that you already feel every emotion to its core. Adding to that, your negative thoughts and experiences of the moment can leave you panting for some air. The best you can do is let go of those crippling emotions. After you have understood and analysed the situation well, let it go. Don't hold on to it. All the thinking that could have been possibly done is already done. There is nothing left to ponder over now. Gather your energy, which you have so frequently invested in others, and deploy it to soothe yourself. If it worked for them, why won't it work for you?

Being an empath, it is only natural that you pick up the vibes and emotions of the other embroiled in a conflict with you and make it your own. Your ability to feel deeply and strive to understand the other's perspective can leave you on the receiving end of things. To avoid this, strike a balance. Identify the emotions which are yours to work on and which belong to the other person. First resolve the conflicts arising in your mind and then move on to deal with your inter-personal conflicts. Cater to yourself first and only then will you be able to gauge the situation well.

It can be tough when you are trying to be an empath. Here are 10 dialogues you can use when trying to stand in the other person's shoe:

   i. I can imagine what you are going through.
  ii. I am there for you.
 iii. You can rely on me.
  iv. I have been there too.
   v. I feel deeply saddened by what happened to you.
  vi. We don't have to talk if you don't want to.
 vii. You can tell me whatever you want to.
viii. It is okay to feel as you are.
  ix. I won't judge.
   x. I have been there where you are. Your reaction is justified.

6

PLEASE, SORRY, THANK YOU!

'It is always so simple, and so complicating, to accept an apology.'

—Michael Chabon

How often do you use these three magical words—please, sorry and thank you? When was the last time you genuinely apologized or heartily said thank you to someone? Has staying cooped up inside your house for long, as the world struggled with the pandemic, cost you your basic conversational etiquette. Maybe it is time to rehearse and bring these three words back into usage. Wouldn't you love to hear the same in return?

Any conversation—no matter how nasty a turn it takes—can be salvaged with a 'please', 'sorry' and 'thank you'. Though it is true that these do not impact what has already taken place, it can at least minimize the harm or the hurt caused. We all learnt the importance of these back in playschool but have sadly become ignorant of its necessity with growing age. We have started overlooking and undermining the importance of these words.

Try asking for a cup of coffee from your sibling. Then try asking your sibling for a glass of water by adding 'please' in your request. Do you not feel the difference? While the former may come across as an order and even result in annoying your sibling, the latter request will be considered without much ado. All it took to make the difference was simply the usage of just one term. This was the most basic example that many of us must have come across in our daily lives. Those who haven't, can try this for an experiment, even with a friend.

These three words also convey to your listener your innermost feelings and what kind of a person you are. It must be remembered that while making use of these words, your present and future actions should reciprocate with the same. These are effectively part of good manners and should be taken for basic etiquette which cannot be done away with or compromised at any cost. These will help you establish a good rapport within your domestic, social and professional circles. These words make for a wholesome conversation and should be used judiciously, as and when needed. A conversation becomes more relaxed with the usage of these words; the possibility of conflicts decreases considerably. This you can try for yourself as an experiment. Go about using none of these magic words in your speech for about a week, and then in the consequent seven days, do the exact opposite. Encourage a friend to do the same. Then note down your observations of your own emotions following the experiment. Take your results and that of your friend; you will notice there are not many differences in what the two of you have to say about your respective emotions. Conversations in the second week of your experiment must have been easier to handle and engage with.

Implementing the usage of these three words in your everyday conversations will make your personality humbler, polite and more attractive to your listeners.

Use Them Generously

There should be nothing holding you back from using the three magic words in your conversation, no matter what the setting. There are no laws and rules to be followed when it comes to using these words. For a more meaningful and peaceful conversation, get into the habit of using these words. They exhibit how down to earth, well-mannered and humble you are as a person. It will earn you the appreciation of others. People remember basic good manners shown by others and that goes a long way in determining your relationship with them.

Start your sentences and end them with a please, sorry, or thank you, wherever you deem fit. You will not run any risk by overly using them, given you do mean what you are saying in the sentences followed by these words. Use them generously, but also with a sense of responsibility. Attempting to mask the hidden interests behind the usage of these words is not very difficult to uncover. Once they are uncovered, you will be done for; also, do not forget the embarrassment that would be caused. Hence, use these words generously, but genuinely.

Encourage Your Children Too

Catch them young. Get them into the early practise of using these three magic words not just while conversing with their elders but also while communicating with their peers. The rules should be the same for everyone. While children are taught about the same at school, the same should also be reinforced while staying at home. Inculcating this habit should not be limited to academic domain but spread out to their personal lives too, which includes their caretakers, playmates and siblings.

While giving initial lessons, refrain from reprimanding them too strongly. A gentle reminder to use the magic words should be enough when you have just started teaching them the importance of their usage in day-to-day life. Also, refrain from reprimanding them on the lack of usage of these words in public; doing so might infuriate and make them a rebel. Things can go south from there. The goal is to inculcate in them good behaviours and not take them away from even the possibility of acquiring one. You must be patient with them.

Parents themselves should follow these rules about saying please, sorry and thank you as well. Children are good imitators and look up to their parents and teachers when it comes to catching phrases and certain parts of speech. If you yourself are far away from using these words, it would be difficult for your kids to learn the same. They tend to follow your footsteps. So, bring about the change in yourself and your child will follow suit. This forms one of the basic lessons that a toddler ought to know at their age. Usage of these three words will help your child stay clear from conflicts with friends, teachers and even with you. Often, children who are not into the habit of saying please, sorry and thank you are the ones reprimanded for unruly behaviour in school.

Most of us have gone through a phase when we had a classmate who would be unapologetic, ungrateful and unruly most of the time. All this student cared for was getting through the day and all the teachers worried about was getting through a day without reprimanding him. There are exceptions everywhere. The student never changed, much to the woe of his teachers and parents.

Don't Hide Behind These Words

Recollecting the usage of the three words generously, but genuinely is necessary as was talked about above. The excessive and uncalled usage might call for judgements from those around. In case you have been using 'please' very frequently in every meeting while communicating with your boss, your colleagues will eventually end up noticing that. It is not necessary and required to end and start a sentence with the word while communicating with your boss or for that matter, any superior. You may run the risk of being labeled a sycophant. People around, noticing your speech, might come under the impression that you are indulging in excessive bootlicking. What you might be viewing as a mere exercise of your good manners can be misunderstood very easily by many if you don't time the usage of these words well.

There are times when one makes a mistake and tries to shove it beneath the word 'sorry'. Hiding behind an apology was never a good option to begin with. Owe your mistake, make up for it. An apology for the same is always welcome but that should not be the end of it. Instead, you can approach the person you have wronged in any way and ask them how would they like you to make amends. If your idea is to apologize, be sure to give a genuine apology, and along with it a redressal to the grievance caused.

Simply putting forth a 'sorry' after a mistake has been committed will not amount to anything good. It is a mere word if one doesn't intend to rectify their actions in any sense. Uttering the word should only be seen as the first step of an apology. Your body language too needs to be expressing how sorry you are. Given your efforts are genuine, your body language will naturally align to your emotions. You will not have to work on it at all.

Remember that the person is going to take some time to forgive you. Do not rush them or overwhelm them with repeated apologies. You have already conveyed how sorry you are. Now it is their time to process the same. How can that not take time? Did you decide overnight to apologize to them for your mistakes. Even that must have taken many nights. So let time be by their side. All you can do, meanwhile, is wait. It might not happen tonight or the next day. It might not be possible for them to accept your apology then and there. This, in turn, should not make you restless. The person is probably trying to forgive and forget, and that can be a time-taking process in itself.

Similarly, while expressing your gratitude to a person, do not do so simply by saying a simple 'thank you'. While mere saying of the words also counts and goes a long way in adding to your inter-personal relationships, finding a way to say thank you will act as cherry on top of a cake. It's always the actions that count. You need not go overboard thinking of novel ways to thank your mother for getting you vacation tickets for your favourite destination. You may do so just by baking her favourite cake or by putting up a thank-you note on her bedpost. Any act done with a kind heart and genuine intentions counts.

Being Humble Can Be New Way of Living

Learn to say the word 'please' while giving orders or issuing directions to someone; use the word 'please' when you are asking them to get some work done. Also, use it while turning down an offer made by someone. To some, this might seem of no consequence or little value, but when used, the word does leave a positive impact.

Start using the word while communicating with the first person you talk to in the beginning of your day. It could be your partner, your sibling, or a milkman. There is nothing revolutionary to be done here. All you are doing is adding a little kindness to your words and being humble. This simple word has the power of clearing misunderstandings, calming flaring tempers, and opening new doors of reconciliation for warring groups or individuals. It makes a sentence softer, simpler and less authoritative (in case some direction is being given). Saying 'please' shows our respect and consideration for the person we are talking to. It can also be seen as an effort on our behalf to better our relationship with the other person. Age is no bar when it comes to using this term. You could be the younger one or the older one making a request to someone older or younger to you and vice-versa.

The benefits to enjoy are surplus. It all trickles down to being able to inculcate the habit of being able to say the word, as and when needed.

Its usage while making a request is known to nearly everyone. However, a mention makes it must for those very few who are oblivious to this. Chances should not be taken in precarious conditions wherein one is trying to impart suitable knowledge to make a mark on one's way of living.

Cross Your Heart First

Be truthful to yourself. Coating your speech with these three magic words just to impress the other will not go a long way in establishing what you are hoping for. If you have your eyes set on winning over the new boss at your workplace, the new student in class, or the new neighbourhood, just throwing in these words causally in conversations would not be of much advantage to you.

These should not be substituted for flattery. Use these words only when you mean to.

Saying sorry without feeling regretful or apologetic in your heart won't translate to the literal meaning of the term. You can always apologize for the mistakes committed in the past. It might have been a year or more; maybe a lot of time has passed away. But if you come to realize your mistakes, go ahead and make a genuine apology. Acceptance or rejection of the same is up to the person you have wronged. Your task should be to offer an apology wholeheartedly and mean it. If you think on a positive note, maybe that person was waiting for a single apology from you…it might end up breaking the ice between you two and bringing your relationship to normalcy again. One should always take such chances.

Same goes for expressing gratitude. When done genuinely, they can motivate, develop trust and improve the relationship of two individuals or groups. For example, if one of the two nations that have been at war for years expresses gratitude to the other for agreeing to de-escalate deployment in forward areas, it would go a long way in strengthening their diplomatic relations. As another example, think of a manager who goes ahead and thanks each of his group members for their contribution to the success of a project. This small act of gratitude will lift up the spirits and motivation level of each one of them. They will feel appreciated and appreciated employees give in their best performance when they are openly valued. A considerate manager is likewise valued by all employees. It becomes a wholesome relationship.

Not Everyone Follows Etiquette

It is not possible to go on correcting others and forcing them to implement the usage of 'please', 'sorry' and 'thank you' in their day-to-day conversations. Ensuring that we stick to the basic etiquette of conversation should be the focus of our concern. We should stay put from participating in the herd mentality; we should be able to distinguish the right from wrong. If others are not used to saying these words as often as you, let that not be an issue of annoyance for you. It is possible that the new workplace you have shifted to lacks the culture of employees using these words in their conversations with their contemporaries but the same people use these terms excessively while talking to their seniors. Such people might be labeled as trucklers by others. You do not have to follow their suit. Stick to your own values and what you believe in. Continue using the three words in your conversations indiscriminately. It is entirely up to you to determine how your communication skills build or ruin your interpersonal relationships.

Usage of 'please', 'sorry' and 'thank you' gains even more importance at a professional set-up where you are supposed to exhibit the best of your work ethics and communication skills. Make sure you use these words while conversing with everyone and not just selected few. The goal should be refined conversations and equal treatment to all.

Strengthening and building up our own conversational skills should come first. We never know who we may end up influencing for the better. If we start ensuring the usage of the three magic words while conversing with people around us, slowly and gradually they will be likely to pick up these words and use them in their own conversations.

Servitude is Archaic

Language should not be used for making anyone feel inferior or to enable anybody in feeling superior. The way you communicate with others should never be influenced by which strata of the society they come from. As mentioned before, the usage of 'please', 'sorry' and 'thank you' should be indiscriminate—you should make use of these words while talking to anyone and everyone without stressing on bias of any sort. This is yet another lesson which the young ones need to be taught at home as well as their schools.

There's no need to not treat someone gently and with kindness just because they conduct your daily errands and are employed by you or your family. Make sure to use the magic words, as and when they help you with a chore, or when you need their help with something. Exercise humility and kindness towards everyone you know. Do not let worn out feelings and hovering negativity from your previous experiences to creep into your conversations. They usually start by manifesting in the form of usage of negative words. Be on a lookout and stay wary of any changes that you feel you are undergoing in your thought process as that would eventually show up in your conversations with others.

Apologizing and expressing gratitude are things best done when done from the heart. For some of those who might be alien to the concept, this is what an apology or thanks can sound like:

i. I am sorry for hurting your emotions.
ii. I am sorry for not taking your advice in consideration.
iii. I'll try to score more the next time. Sorry for this year's results.

iv. Sorry for not being there for you.
v. I am sorry that you had to go to the party by yourself.
vi. Thank you for the amazing birthday present.
vii. Thank you for looking after my kid.
viii. Thank you for cooking this delicious food.
ix. Thank you for helping me out with the pending work.
x. Thank you for not leaving my side when I was throwing tantrums.

7

NOT ALL SPEAK ALIKE

*'Optimism is the faith that leads to achievement.
Nothing can be done without hope and confidence.'*

—Helen Keller

The mere idea of going up on that stage, in front of a hundred odd faces, to recite a poem has been terrifying to quite some of us as a child. Many overcame this fear as they advanced to adulthood. For some, it became a deep-seated problem. The fear remained and along with it came another trouble.

What might start as stage fright escalates slowly into a speech impairment—stammering. It can affect any of us; for some the effects on day-to-day life might be minimal, for others it can be disastrous. It is inhibiting, nonetheless. The severity is entirely subjective. Initiating conversations, be it on one-on-one basis over the call, or in person becomes a tough task. It can impact you in your childhood and even in your teenage years. No matter when it strikes, the effects can be felt throughout one's life.

What is seemingly a good thing to do for many people, becomes a hurdle for those who struggle with stammering. Engaging in a conversation at workplace, showing up at family gatherings and holiday meet-ups becomes taxing on their minds.

The speed and fluency of their speech doesn't remain in tandem with the flow of their thoughts. They halt once, they halt twice, trying to put their chain of thoughts, their views into words. Communication at any level, any forum becomes food for negative thoughts then.

It is only natural to find yourself scared to participate in events of little or larger significance if you find yourself stammering and often struggling to open conversations. The good news is that with consistent attempts at improvising your speech and getting rid of the stutter to a large extent, you can end up overcoming this hurdle that has caused you immense discomfort throughout your life. While the road to recovery could be shorter for some, for others, it might be a long way. The focus should entirely remain on the end goal, i.e., the ability to talk without stammering. You can practise speaking by yourself standing in front of a mirror, while talking to a friend, or by taking speech therapy sessions. Always keep an open mind when it comes to remedies. One doesn't know what one might end up benefitting from.

It might be a matter of months or years—varies from individual to individual. Many causes have been enlisted for stammering. While some attribute it to emotional trauma in childhood, others point at neuromuscular complications as the reason behind why one starts stammering.

Mirror Mirror, on the Wall!

Many have practised this technique. It is tried and tested. Simply stand in front of a mirror, stare at yourself as you talk. Observe everything about you—right from the pitch of your voice, to your facial expressions, to your body language. Make a note of everything. What is it that you feel needs an improvement? You are your best judge. Become your audience.

Quite often, people who stammer tend to have a poor body language. The word often has been used because such might not be the case with everybody who struggles with the problem. These people tend to stoop a lot while sitting or standing and have a sluggish walk at times. If you can relate with these statements, why not try changing these aspects about yourself? Doing so will eventually result in a positive transformation in yourself, which will be visible to all.

Go to that mirror on the wall again. Watch yourself walk, sit and stand. Change your stance; look yourself in the eye and remind yourself that there is nothing that cannot be achieved with practise. You have suffered enough and now is the time to overcome your challenges. Transforming yourself into a confident person cannot be an overnight process. So, learn to be patient with yourself. Frustration is obvious but you must not give up the path you have chosen now.

Once you start with your daily practise, you will come to observe certain facial expressions which, even before you stammer, give you away; it explicitly expresses your discomfort and fear around the possibility of getting stuck on a word or a letter. Work on that expression. Do away with it if you must. If it is preceded by stammering, it is likely that you will see a considerable impact on the latter with a reduction of the former. Do this every day for maybe 15 minutes. It will be like you conducting your own therapy sessions. What else in the world can be better? This will also help you control your facial expressions after you end up stammering. Try not to be very disappointed in yourself or feel sorry for the incident. Brush it aside and move ahead to the next word or the next sentence. Pausing in between to think over and analyse the word or the letter that made you stammer will only make the situation worse. It will make you even more self-conscious. So, stop self-criticizing.

Take Deep Breaths in Between

It is okay to get stuck even when on the road to recovery. When you find yourself struggling with a word or a letter, pause and take a deep breath. Clear out all thoughts of self-criticism and self-pity. Simply focus on that long inhalation followed by a deep exhalation. Repeat this number of times; repeat this till you feel better. It is okay to take your time as you catch your breath. You can excuse yourself from the audience and take out time for yourself in that moment.

This will help you calm your nerves and relax. You need to let go of the built-up stress and paranoia around putting forth your ideas and thoughts in front of a bunch of people, no matter how close or alien to you. You can continue with your conversation after you have taken some quiet time for yourself and gathered yourself together. It is your own battle, and what others think of it and how they evaluate you should be the last thing on your mind.

The idea here is to help yourself relax in case of a stressful situation. While there is no scientific evidence that breathing will help you get rid of stammering, let alone cure it, deep breathing can offer you a pause and allow you to refocus on the thoughts you need to convey. It becomes necessary at times to help you get over the stutter and get back to your chain of thoughts. It is not meant to interfere with the flow of your speech but to help you overcome any unwanted pauses while talking. It is not an inhibitor.

To reduce your stress level that tends to trigger your stammer, you can even opt for some yoga exercises. Once the strain and anxiety linked to conversing—be it in the form of public speaking or telephonic communication—is minimized, more than half the work will be done.

Phone a Friend

Call up a friend you are close to, or try to pay them regular visits. Ask them if they can help you out by listening to you talk. Often what we need is a patient listener and one in whose presence we won't feel judged and criticized. Feel free to be yourself. This is after all your own person, the one you trust. Even if you fumble, you can always pick up from there and give it another try. You have their faith in you. Stop being hard on yourself; if not done so, it will only make things tougher for you. You can practise your communication skills with this person. Ask them to give you feedbacks on which aspect they feel you should work on; ask them whether it is your contradicting chain of thoughts, incoherency in your views, a timid body language; they will surely come up with points that will help you in the long run.

You can let go of the fear of criticism and your paranoia around talking in front of someone and putting forth your ideas without stammering. This is your practise session, and the one in front of you is your cheerleader, they are your supporter. Do not fear them. You can also approach a close family member with the same request. You need a cushion to fall back on every time you fall, till you learn to stand upright on your own after taking a fall. This, again, can be a time taking process, and should not be rushed.

While talking to a close one, you won't feel half the anxiety and consciousness you experience while talking in a group of new or unknown people. Hence, the former lot makes for the best practise group for you. Form a routine which works the best for both parties. You must be considerate of their time table while you seek their help. Stick to the plan, but be flexible about it, as and when needed. The person might not be available every time you need them to. And that is okay.

It is with repeated practise sessions that you will be able to diminish your fear of speaking in front of others. As the next step in the training, you can ask the person to invite some of their acquaintances. It will make for a good mock practise session. You can give a little impromptu speech or invite everyone for a discussion on a topic of general interest.

Panic Is No Good

So, you ended up stammering in front of your colleagues while giving a presentation. As much as you force yourself into believing that it is the end of the world, it really is not. It is just another bad experience from which you can learn. Make a note of what was the first thing that triggered the stammering in that instance. Work on eliminating those actions or chain of thoughts that caused the incident. The first step would be forcing yourself into making those changes. Maybe, instead of looking at a person or two throughout the entire meeting, you need to start being more inclusive. Try to not focus on selected people and look at them for longer period of time during the course of your speech; perhaps, that is what is triggering your nervousness. Give everybody equal attention. Maintain your body language, such that it is inclusive of everybody and not dependant on a few.

Thinking about that moment again and again will only give rise to your anxiety level, which in turn, will affect your speech even more. Forget and move on to the next word or the next sentence you have in mind.

If you are prone to panicking, why not try giving a mock interview or a mock viva a day or two before the actual event. This will help you prepare beforehand and give you some assurance about your preparedness. You can do the mirror practise or gather a fake audience to deliver your speech to. Go through the content that you have to present in front of others. In case you come across any triggering words or ones that you find difficult to utter, try going for their synonyms. Every problem comes with a solution. You just need to keep yourself calm and composed. Fidgeting and panicking, as you do now, tends to make things worse.

Change the Situation

If you realize that there are certain situations that are bound to make you stammer, try to change those situations. While this may not be a productive solution every time, you can try doing so at times. If you know that reaching your performance venue after the bar is full makes you nervous and leaves you stammering during your stand-up gig, you should consider arriving at the venue much earlier. This will help you get acquainted with your surroundings and most importantly, the stage. While this might not eliminate your trouble completely, it is bound to diminish it to a great extent.

Another example can be giving a speech in front of an

assembly of the student body of your school. If the mere thought of it leaves you in sweat, and you are scared about ending up stammering in front of everyone, why not try giving the same speech in front of your friends first? Their support can be comforting and leave a calming effect on you—exactly what you are in need of. You will have a smaller version of the assembly for your practise. Some situations might not always be in your control, but if given a thought to, there are some situations that can be controlled by you. All you need to do is put in that extra effort to make the circumstances a lot less stressful for you.

Often, one makes the mistake of imagining what we would be like in a particular situation. We build up scenarios and put ourselves in the spotlight. We assume how we would end up reacting in that situation—the assumption tends to be on the negative side. We draw inferences from our past experiences and impose them on the present scenario. By doing so, we end up getting trapped in a loop of chain reactions where nothing productive ever takes place. If such is the case with you, you need to get out of those imaginary situations. Step outside and walk into the real world. You need to shift your focus to the situation awaiting you in the real world; put your energy and attention into the present moment.

Exhibit Patience

You may have come across many people who get visibly nervous during public speaking and end up stammering. There must have been many who struggled to initiate a conversation or got stuck at a particular word. What was your reaction to such situations back then? Did you lose interest in the conversation or looked forward for it to get over soon?

When being a listener, your role in a conversation does not become passive. It is with your constant acknowledgment and attention to the speaker that the conversation goes on in a healthy way. Your role only increases in its importance when you are interacting with someone who knowingly stammers. You need to exhibit patience while hearing them talk as they attempt to get their ideas across without stammering. They are putting their best efforts in order to carry on with the conversation; you, by all means, should reciprocate those efforts.

Do not try to get ahead of them if they get stuck at some word or letter; don't try to finish or complete a sentence for them. All you should and must do is wait. Just wait for them to get over the stammer and continue with what they were saying. You must not 'help' them or make them feel any different. It can prove to be frustrating for them; would you appreciate others putting your thoughts into words before you are able to articulate them yourself?

Do not break eye contact with them for that will lower their confidence to continue with their sentence and the conversation would remain incomplete.

You must realize that it can be frustrating for anyone to suddenly stammer while articulating their thoughts. This, in turn, can add up to their social anxiety making the situation even worse for them. You don't have to come to their rescue as you are not needed to. All you are needed to do is to stand by their side patiently. That will go a long way in helping them soothe their anxiety.

Those who stammer might not be able to express their views in the first go. The biggest tip for you—the listener—can be to be patient and let them finish what they are saying. REFRAIN from saying any of the listed things:

i. Since when have you been stammering?
ii. Is this what you meant?
iii. Which is the letter that you get stuck at the most?
iv. Do you have it since birth?
v. Is it only you in your family who stammers?
vi. Have you tried seeing a speech therapist yet?
vii. Do you try talking standing in front of a mirror?
viii. Perhaps, the root cause is social anxiety.
ix. Are you made fun of whenever you get stuck at a word?
x. It must be frustrating not being able to speak without stammering.

8

TALKING AFTER A LONG WHILE

'The scariest thing about distance is that you don't know whether they'll miss you or forget you.'

—Nicholas Sparks

You might be seeing your friend after as long as a decade. They now have a family of their own and so do you. The last time you two met each other was when you were applying for jobs. You two have come a long way since then, growing up and maturing in life. Things are bound to have changed now; there might be some pleasant and some not so pleasant changes for you to notice.

The venue has been set, the date has been fixed and you are finally looking forward to meeting this friend of yours whom you last saw a long time ago. Your focus shifts to how would they find your personality; you suddenly become self-conscious. You start thinking of all the things you have to talk about, all the tragedies, happiness and the misfortunes you have to share with them. That makes you wonder whether they spent their lives well and lived happily. You feel overwhelmed and concerned. Suddenly, the wait seems endless.

All sorts of possible conversation starters run across your

mind. Should you ask them about how they are or inquire about the kids and the spouse first? Should you offer them a seat first or welcome them with a warm hug? You leave that for the time being. What were your common interests, what was it that both of you enjoyed? That might seem to be a question tough to answer for you cannot recall well. You start thinking of all the things they liked and enjoyed talking about—though the focus is on having a natural conversation, you still don't mind noting down certain points.

You might feel some awkwardness and nervousness in finding out whether the two of you still share the same bond as you used to, a decade ago. It is only natural to wonder who will be able to break the ice first. Starting a conversation—barring the initial small talk—might seem like a task to accomplish in the beginning. You can stick to certain points and retain them in your mind while communicating with them. It would help keep the conversation going without much ado.

Why not concentrate solely on creating lasting memories of your get-together, putting any tension to the side? Here are some ways which will keep your conversation going on. These may not be necessarily followed in the order they are written. See what works best for you. The example of two friends meeting after a long time has been considered.

How Have You Been?

Ask them about how they have been doing. A simple 'how have you been' or 'I haven't seen you in ages' can be good starters. You can keep it simple and straightforward; the conversation will unfold smoothly. There is no need of stressing over what be the perfect conversation starter. This is the person you have known for a long time. Do not let time and distance create any awkwardness amidst you and them.

This can work as an appropriate ice breaker. Ask them how their parents are, how the kids and the spouse are doing. This will not only show your concern, but also express your interest in their life. What is the last thing you remember about their families—initiate the conversation from there.

You need not base the entire conversation on their family. You may take an update on how they have been doing since the last time you met them. For instance, why not talk about the last Christmas when you met up with their parents and shared a meal together? Take a walk down the memory lane. If you met them last time when their child was only a year old, ask about how his schooling is going on, ask them about how parenthood is treating them.

There must be a lot to share and know about what all happened in each others' lives since the last time you met. You can share details about your family too. It is a conversation and not a question-answer session. Make the conversation as lively as possible. This is no interview after all.

Offer Compliments

You have met them after a long while. There must be several changes you would have noticed about them by now. It need not be said that you must try to talk about 'positive changes'. What is the first thing you noticed about them, is it their outfit or the hairstyle that suits them? The tiniest of details can make for a good compliment. It will also make the other person feel noticed and valued. Doing so can offer a start for a smooth conversation. However, make sure not to overdo it. Another point that you ought to remember is that you shouldn't go on inquiring about the details of what you complimented them for. For example, if they are sporting an attractive hairdo, don't go on asking about how much they spent on it and which hair salon did they opt for. Such questions can tend to be spoilers for the conversation ahead. In the worst possible situation, the other person might take offence for the cross questioning. Hence, give a compliment and then move on.

Refrain from asking them whether something is real. If you notice them using a branded cosmetic product, try complimenting them about how the colour suits them instead of questioning them about the authenticity of the product, simply because it is an expensive choice. Not only doing the latter be rude on your behalf, it will also jeopardize your rapport with the person. It may cause them shame and alter the direction of your talk.

Offering a compliment is not just a good conversation starter when you are meeting someone after a long while, this can also be used when you meet someone informally for the first time. Refrain from using this in formal set-ups like interviews or situations where you are bound to be analysed on the basis of what you say and talk about. You can also dig into some information about them before you meet. It could be regarding anything, right from their areas of interest to their favourite genres of movies. You can compliment them for their likes and choices. They might be having certain traits you are fond of and always have been. A compliment need not be made solely in the beginning of a conversation or be used as an ice breaker; you can offer some of those even in between an ongoing conversation. There is no perfect or suitable timing set to compliment the other. It is not a difficult task to accomplish.

There are various things for which you can compliment them. It can even be regarding an idea they bring to the table or simply their way of thinking. Tell them that their ideas amaze you; make them feel appreciated. Give those compliments only when you genuinely mean them, lest it would be seen as a means to an end.

When being complimented, always reply with a thank you instead of making a haughty comment. If you are complimented for your choice of outfit for an occasion, do not proceed with 'I invested a lot of time and money on this dress.' Be humble when being complimented. The ideal case scenario is if you can reciprocate their compliment with one of your own.

Give in to Nostalgia

Revisit memories of the days and the time you spent together. What is it that you two enjoyed doing the most? Was it bunking lectures or was it going for a shopping spree after exams? Was it going for ice cream treats every now and then or was it the last Halloween where you dressed up as Superman and could barely scare anyone? Talk about those days. Talk about all the common friends you had, how great a time it was. Take a walk down the memory lane and take them along. It is bound to bring back some bittersweet memories. This is the nostalgia for the days gone by; let those memories come back with full force. Laugh together, or cry if you must. It is all about reliving those moments once again after all these years. Nostalgia can be a healthy way to reconnect with someone you once were close with and want to establish closeness with, once again. It will help you remind how the two of you came to know each other and how you ended up bonding with one another. Do not fret over the emotional floodgates it might open eventually. Go with the flow of the conversation.

Anything around you can be a reminder of a past incident. Feel free to talk about that memory with them. It might be the food the person on the table next to you is having; that might be a reminder of how you always hated it but eventually came to like it after your friend cooked it for you once. It might be a song playing nearby at which you performed in your graduation party. The students walking past the school gate splashing in puddles on that rainy day might remind you of your own school days. The yellow woollen scarf worn by a child sitting next to you might be similar to a birthday present you gave years ago. Cherish such memories. There may be several instances like these just floating around and waiting to be noticed. Not that you should not focus on the person in front of you, but why not also try to be receptive of the environment around you; you may end up finding many clues that can act as a link to the days gone by. You can also discuss about the best thing that has happened to both of you in all these years. Share with them what made you happy or even what made you cry. Tell them everything you would have told them, had you not lost touch over the years. Now is the chance. On a side note, do not try to make it entirely about yourself.

You can talk about a specific day in particular which was important for the both of you. Ask them how much do they remember about that day. On the basis of their reply, continue your conversation in as friendly manner as possible. Keep in mind that there is also a chance that they do not recall the days and the moments you very clearly do. Do not hold grudges against them for such a simple reason.

However, be sure not to bring back incidents that are likely to bring feelings of disdain and discomfort. You have met the other person after considerable time, and thus, it would not be wise to initiate discussion on a topic which is bound to create an atmosphere of tension between you two. It was, after all, definitely not for the purpose of uncovering old wounds that you decided to meet them. Focus on the pleasant memories and ones that bring about happy tears, smiles and laughter.

There must have been a reason why the two of you were not in touch for all this while. There is no use of pondering over why and how that happened. Delving into this part of your past will not evoke nostalgia but is more likely to give way to bitterness and awkwardness between the two of you. Hence, avoid initiating a discussion on that aspect of your shared past.

Find Common Ground

There must be something common between the two of you to talk about. A favourite movie, a book, an author, shopping destination, a dish, a flower—it could be anything. It might be all about being able to remember what the two of you enjoyed the most and liked equally. It is not difficult for friends to find a common ground to talk about. Once those similarities are recollected, start a conversation. You can ask whether they still are fond of the things they enjoyed a long time back. Ask as many related open-ended questions. Indulge in a friendly banter; don't keep the talks limited to a question-answer session. Once they are done talking about how they still like that dish you talked about or how they have grown that favourite flower in a garden back home, you can reply with your own take on those similarities and whether you are still fond the way you once were or has that changed for the good or the worse. Share your stories with one another.

It might be a possibility that the two of you have drastically changed over the years. Your taste, liking, favourites might have changed too. That should, however, not act as a deterrent in your conversation; it should not act as a spoiling agent. Embrace the fact that with time, circumstances change and so do people. But it should not mean that you are left disappointed and at a loss of words. You should not start treating them as an alien entity and give way to awkwardness. Growing up is just a part of life and also the beauty of it. You too, must have seen several chances in varied aspects of your life in the past few years since the last time the two of you met. If you can accept the newness life brought you at every stage, you should be able to accept the person in front of you too.

If you sense that a lot has changed about their personality, refrain from making any sarcastic remark or saying anything hurtful. The person in front of you is the same you once knew; they only have some newer traits, a newer aura around themselves now. It might be that they never wanted to step into parenthood but are now a parent of four. Rather than being shocked and surprised at how their life turned out to be, congratulate them on becoming a parent. Dig into the details about the kids; ask for their names, photographs, the hobbies they engage in. Be warm and welcoming. Give them the confidence that they can share right about anything with you without facing any judgement. Gauge all the newness that has entered in their lives and talk about them—ask and ask. This will express your interest in their present life and not just in the good old days gone by.

Come Back to the Present

The memories of the past must be dear and close to your heart. No doubt, you wish to relive them again and again and discuss it at lengths. Reminiscing is common when you meet someone after a very long time. How you remember them and how they have remembered you all this time surely moves the two of you. Treasure your memories and keep them safe, tucked away in your heart. That is the foundation of the kind of bond you two will have in the present and continue having in the future. The past is important for sure, but let us try moving a bit ahead.

But let that not become an excuse to not talk of the present. After walking down the memory lane, it is time to step into the present and acquaint yourselves with what has been happening in each others' lives. A simple catching-up among friends. There must be a lot to talk about and share when it comes to new experiences, new lessons that you learnt in all these years.

Ask them what have they been up to lately; what keeps them busy; how is the job going; is the construction of the new house coming along well? You might have known them well, once upon a time, but it is time to know them all over again—there are many new aspects in their lives that can be talked about. Bombarding them with questions one after the other can be pretty exhausting for them to answer. So, keep it slow and conversational. As they tell you something new, talk about what has been the latest development in your life as well. Tell them about the all the new people whom you've met lately in your life and how many new friends you've made. Tell them about how stressful it seems to juggle between office work and household chores. Keep it chatty. Make it about the both you, not just you, and not just them.

Ask them about their likes and dislikes given they have a different taste now regarding a lot of things. Get to know them once again as you used to. Keep in mind that their likes and dislikes might have changed but they are inherently the same person you once knew. Don't hesitate in reconnecting with them or finding a means to connect over new experiences they have had. It can open new avenues for even better conversations. You will have various topics to talk about—it will include not just the past but the present too. So, make the most of it. Show genuine interest in their present life and what all have they seen change since the last time you met. People can easily pick up when the other person is really being genuine or simple faking to appear so.

Be Cautious of What Hurts

While you go on with your conversation, try not to dig further into certain topics. It can be easily understood by one's body language when they are uncomfortable regarding an issue. Be on a lookout for those signs. They might be trying to avoid eye contact, they might be shifting positions in their chair, or they might have crossed their arms suddenly. There can be many such signs which indicate that they are not comfortable talking about a particular incident of their life. There are certain memories and incidents in life we try to avoid recalling again or discussing about. It tends to bring with it old wounds that you worked on healing for a long time. Such memories are better left unattended. A lot must have happened over all this time you didn't meet this person; there must be many tragic incidents too, which you don't wish to talk about. Same goes for them. Not anything and everything needs to be brought out in the open. As the conversation continues, you will understand the topics they are trying to avoid and let go of. Respect their choices and don't pursue what they don't wish to discuss.

Asking further questions or being inquisitive about something they are not comfortable with will only aggravate the discomfort, and in the worst-case scenario, might put an end to your conversation. The goal should be to have a comfortable conversation wherein both of you discuss and talk about things you like, admire and appreciate. There is no need to venture into topics that can spoil the mood of the conversation. For example, if your friend underwent a painful separation from their spouse, the details of which you know, refrain from initiating a discussion on that topic. There is no point in talking about a chapter in one's life which is only bound to bring sorrow and grief. Similarly, if you know that they recently got fired from their job, do not go on seeking details of what exactly happened and why. If there is a sensitive topic they would like to talk about, they would take the first step. If they don't, then they don't wish to.

Be swift to change a topic if you notice your friend being uncomfortable answering any questions relating to it. There are many topics the two of you have a chat one. So, switch to the next topic without making it very obvious to them. You might be having their best interest at heart while you start off a conversation about something that hurt them in the past. Perhaps, you are trying to get them a closure as a friend. Perhaps, you are trying to come to their rescue. But it should be understood that they will reach out to you if they need a helping hand or they need to be saved. All you can and should do is wait for them to talk about that difficult chapter of their life. If they don't, it simply means that they are trying to stay away from bringing back those memories. You can help them here by not recalling those old wounds.

It is possible that you wish to confront your friend for something that took place in the past. Under such a situation, you need to ask yourself whether it is really a pressing matter that needs to be discussed right away. Can it not wait for the next time when you meet them? The two of you have after all met after a considerable gap and bringing up issues which might cause pain and hurt should be avoided. It is better to make happy memories than fixate on the old ones which were exactly the opposite.

Make Future Plans

Don't make it your last meeting with them. Plan when you would like to see them again. Don't make it sound like a casual suggestion. Discuss at lengths, how the two of you can meet up again sometime soon. Decide the date, time and venue. Make efforts to stay in touch with them; take the initiative. Work out a time that would be convenient for the both of you. If the two of you live in different cities, or countries for that matter, decide mutually who out of the two of you can cover a larger distance. Discuss the feasibility. Don't impose your decisions on them; arrive at them mutually. Try not to expect things to be hunky dory all the time. Always consider unexpected outcomes.

This would show the person that you are interested in maintaining the closeness with them that you once shared. Not only is it a good way to end a conversation, it also expresses the importance you give to them. It would show how grateful and happy you were to finally meet the person after all these years.

Why not plan the next meet-up with both of your families

in attendance? This way you would get to know more about them and get to be more involved in their lives. Or maybe you can plan a larger get-together with all of your mutual and new friends joining in.

There might be a possibility that the two of you met this one time seeking a closure and the meeting ended with a confrontation about a much-dreaded issue. Under such circumstances, being able to decide to meet up again can be tough and maybe unimaginable in some situations. Do not force your decision upon the other person. If they are equally interested in meeting you, they would give you the hints in the course of the conversation.

You Can Even Message Them

Do not forget about the good old written communication. In the times of instant messaging and emails, you can definitely connect with that long-lost friend using either of the two. Getting a chance to stay in touch with someone you met or were close with a long time ago cannot become any easier than this. All you need to do is muster up some courage and send them your good wishes saying you miss them. Just a heartfelt message can do the job.

A simple 'I was thinking about you' or 'it has been a long time since we last met' can be a good start for getting back in touch with them. If you came to know about some congratulatory news about them, drop in your good wishes along with asking how they have been doing.

Another way of trying to contact someone again can be by sending them a picture of yourself or maybe a picture of the two of you together from the past. That will help them reconnect with the old memories and make them give a prompt reply. You can even send them a picture that reminds you of them or a memory of the two of you together. It will show that you still keep them in your thoughts and can be a warm gesture for an ice breaker.

It can be nerve wracking when you are waiting for someone to send a reply, given you were apprehensive about sending it the first place. It is understood that you put in a lot of efforts to draft that message checking and rechecking again and again to make sure it sounded genuine and earnest. If possible, after you send them a message or an email, try to forget about it. Occupy yourself with other chores as that will help you take off your mind from the constant anxiety of whether the person will reply or not. You have done what you could and now the ball is in their court. All you can do is sit and wait. But don't centre your life around that waiting period.

At times, people drift apart for varied reasons. However, let that not become a reason to stop you from texting them if you have been thinking of them lately. If the situation you two were in the last time was not a healthy one, then you can leave behind an open-ended message for them— 'Hi! I was just wondering what your life is like these days. I'd love to catch up.' Make it simple and to the point. However, don't sit back hoping for them to reply immediately. They might not be on the same page as you. They might choose to reply you after some time or even not reply at all. Be ready for any reaction. Perhaps, they were not expecting to hear from you after all this while. It is only human for them to be shocked and surprised. Do not be disheartened though. You tried all that you could. Communication is a two-way process and with just you being in the frame will not suffice. So, step outside from the picture now.

Following are some communication starters you can use when meeting someone a long while.

i. I am glad we finally got the chance to meet again.
ii. I don't remember the last time I saw your face.
iii. You look even better than before!
iv. How have you been all this while?
v. I hope you faced no trouble getting here?
vi. How is everyone back home?
vii. Have you got accustomed to the weather there?
viii. What did you miss the most about this place?
ix. I can't believe it's been 11 years already!
x. You haven't changed one bit.

9

USING COMMUNICATION FOR IMPACT

'You can't use up creativity. The more you use, the more you have.'

—Maya Angelou

To be able to keep someone glued to the conversation, you have to ensure that there is no dull moment in your speech and in what you disseminate. You will have to rack your brain to come up with novel ways to keep that audience of yours amused and entertained.

Why not take a clue from your politicians. Ever witness an assembly of supporters being addressed by their leader? Isn't there a wave of enthusiasm running across the entire gathering with each person bubbling with great gusto? Ever wondered how do they stand, shout and support their leader with an unending fervour and zest? They derive their energy and vivacity from the leader, from the one who is up there on the stage engaging them in a speech that has left them spellbound. What exactly does the leader utter? He is addressing the people standing in front of him as one. He has unified them under a cause.

He has used his intellect and ability to go to the roots of an issue to connect with these people. His words have the effect of urgency in them. He is not talking about himself and his personal agenda, he is talking about their all-round wellbeing. He seeks from them to know what ails them; he promises to eradicate their troubles and anything that comes in the way of their development. He has given them the assurance that come what may, he will stand by their side and work for their progress and rights till his last breath. He has made himself indispensable by becoming available to each and every person he is addressing. He knows how to grab their attention and he has managed to do that effectively. The assembly has erupted into a thunder of claps and cheering.

Speeches like these undergo a lot of research, thinking and creativity to finally arrive at what works best. It is a cumbersome task, not something which is established in a night. The leader has to know how to get his message across and through the hearts of so many, else his speech and agenda would become null and void. We can say he was able to communicate well with each present in the assembly.

You may not have a large assembly of supporters to engage with, but it cannot be denied that several of our day-to-day conversations can be very crucial in determining your future prospects at times—be it about career, your mental wellbeing, or inter-personal relationship with the other person in question. Some conversations need to be indulged in with a pragmatic perspective. You need to weigh in the pros and cons of what you are about to say. Every word has to be measured in-depth for what it stands for. When trying to have an effective conversation and one that benefits you and to some extent, the other, you need to be creative with your thought process and what you put out in words. Try to process and refine what comes to mind first, and base your arguments on known facts.

There are numerous ways in which you can improve your communication skills, make it more powerful and inclusive. Even utilizing communication as your most powerful tool, you can have an impact. For that, you need to be surrounded by people who can help you fulfil that goal in the long run or at least help you move in that direction.

Ask People about Their Greatest Challenges

Ask people what their biggest challenges in life have been. It is a great conversation starter and shows the other person that you take interest in their life.

However, tread with caution, keeping in mind that not many would agree to narrate their life ordeals. Respect their silence and move on. The reason behind their silence could be anything and they do not owe you any explanation. You should not pester them with questions as doing so might carve out an old wound for them, something which will harm them emotionally. So, walk away. They have overcome that hurdle with great difficulty and wish to forget it in order to move ahead in life.

But listen to those who tell you their stories. In it, there might be more for you to take than you can imagine. You get to learn a lot about people from what they fear and what their greatest hurdles have been in life. Such a conversation would not only let you have a look into the events that shaped the person in front of you, but also, offer you an insight into how they have survived what many could not. Conversations that are rich in experience can always be beneficial for you.

What they have suffered in the face of tragedies—be it personal or professional—can teach you a thing or two too. You should learn from those people who have seen and been through a lot in life. Talk to them about how they passed every hurdle and what it took them to survive it all. Try to understand where they come from and what their roots are. Imagine their entire life in one frame, and pick the pieces that help you understand parts of your own life. You can draw from their life, experiences and lessons that can be retold again and again. If it is something that needs to be spread among the masses, seek for their permission first. You may choose to be a disseminator of their stories, but only if they give you their approval.

Asking them about their troubles should not be only about seeking their experience, but also a way for you to offer them help any way you could. It would help you form a connection with them. If you approach a bomb blast victim hoping to get some information from them regarding the incident, it can be a tough task. They might not be on the right frame of mind to be able to divulge details of any importance to you or anybody else. Your intentions for communicating to them might be good; perhaps, all you are looking forward to is to be able to get them justice. But keep their mental state in consideration. You must persevere for a while. At last, if you are not in a position to help them, get them in touch with a person who can do something productive for them and come up with a practical solution.

In another instance, you might be a journalist seeking to write a piece on army veterans, for which you need their inputs. You need to take to the readers what these veterans must have undergone on the field, fighting for their lives and those of their countrymen. Yours is the need to communicate their story. But it should be kept in mind that some of the army veterans might not be willing to come up with their stories. They are probably trying to avoid the nightmarish flashbacks and related trauma. Don't coerce them into talking. Using communication as a tool is of no use if it does not involve mutual parties participating in the conversation willingly.

Ask Them about Their Success Stories

If you know someone who has seen a lot of success and fame in their life, why not delve into their past story. First, read up on their interests and achievements and then go up for a conversation. It is always good to know about a person in advance to some extent before you expect to start a healthy conversation with them. You can start by asking what was the motivation behind their achievement and how did they ace it. What you need to keep in mind is that at times, such questions can be taken in a negative sense and can spoil the course of your conversation. Be very careful of the words you choose to express interest in their story. Do not sound haughty and jealous at any point. You have approached them because they inspire you. Let them know that they've been a big inspiration to you. Express your happiness at being able to meet them in person.

When the initial pleasantries are exchanged, you can pose some questions to them. Observe how comfortable they are with divulging details of their past, and on the basis of that, move ahead with your questions. Stay an active listener. It can be understood if excitement takes control of you while hearing about some incident of their life, but do not interrupt them while they are speaking. They are giving you their life story at your behest. Be respectful to them and thankful for their choice to engage in a conversation with you. You are privy to their personal stories now.

Of the many questions you can ask them, one can be 'what is the best decision you made in your professional life?' Their answer might benefit you. Here, you are listening to a success story about a person who inspires you. There will definitely be many lessons to draw from their experiences. Further ask questions, the answers of which you seek for your own betterment. 'What did you do about time-management' and 'what is your greatest strength' are some examples of the sort of questions you can ask them. Be sure to get the answers from them.

It is not possible that whatever you listen and take away from the conversation will be of absolute use and significance to you. You will have to see for yourself that to which extent can you benefit from the lessons taken from the talk. Each person has their own individuality, and trying to copy someone else to climb the ladder of success might be a very good idea. Think practically. It is okay for you to be overwhelmed after having a conversation with someone you admire and seek inspiration from. But blindly following their path may not be a very wise decision to make.

By now, you know what worked best for them. You had an extensive conversation where he gave you an insider's look into his life. Now, sit back and think about the factors that you can actually start working on, hoping to be as successful as they are someday. You may take hints and cues from their talk but do not try to create replicas and hope for the exact same results. It won't work out.

For example, if your source of inspiration is a famous yoga guru and you aspire to be a psychology professor one day, you need not leave your academics and venture out on his career path. You can for sure rely on certain of his life experience, like why he opted to become a yoga guru in the first place. If they did so with the goal of being able to help people overcome the anxiety and stress of modern life, then there is something for you to note here. Perhaps, you too look forward to disseminate knowledge regarding human mind and behaviour. Here, you have found a similarity and thus you should be able to relate to the 'why' of their career path. However, if you wish to become an architect, for example, what the yoga guru says to you in the conversation might not be entirely useful to you. You have two separate paths after all.

The crux is that, let an influential story or person impact you only when you know that they will take you in the right direction and closer to your goals in life.

Ask People about Their Everyday Struggles

We can refer to the example of the leader from the start of the chapter. Connecting with people on the basis of their everyday struggles and difficulties is a great way to establish your presence amongst them. They need someone who they can communicate with and someone who will lend an ear to their woes. Be that person for them. Use the power of words to make an impact in the lives of others. Be the bridge they need, to link with those who can act on their concerns. Only if you arrive with the promise of being able to help them and the confidence that you will be able to make a positive difference will you be able to establish your presence.

Take this as an instance—if you are working on assimilating information about the sanitation facilities of a village in India and talk to the women folk living there, they are likely to tell you about their harrowing experiences. But you will not get to hear any of their narratives in the first go. For this, you must be patient and work on getting acquainted with them. It is imperative that you understand where they are coming from and how much time they will need to open up to a stranger. It is only natural for them to try to shun you. This will only make your task tougher. But it is for the bigger picture that you must show some patience.

Communicate with them for a while on smaller issues and ones which do not concern them directly. The idea is to not put them in the limelight in the first go. This might make them uncomfortable and upset. Learn about their boundaries. You will eventually get your breakthrough. Once they gain trust in you, they will share their narratives. Listen with great alertness what their narratives have to offer. Also, try not to make the conversation a one-way routine.

As they tell you about their hurdles, ask them further questions; this will encourage them to speak. Let these voices not go unheard. You have with you, what you wanted. You have with you, the experiences of the women who have suffered due to open defecation for a long time. Try to bring about a change. They communicated their woes to you and now it is on you to take this dialogue further where it can be actively worked upon and dealt with. Try to be a harbinger of positive changes using the tool of communication. The knowledge that you have encompassed with your persistent efforts should not go to waste—neither for yourself nor for the women you talked to.

While seeking to know about the everyday problems being faced by others, go with an informed mind. Have the basic knowledge about what is it that ails them. If you expect them to narrate their ordeals to you from the start to the end, then it might not be a possibility. Do your homework diligently. It is after all understood that you need a conversation starter first, to be able to communicate with them. And this cannot be done if you approach with absolutely no knowledge about their existing condition or the situation they are in. They will be quick to dismiss you and not acknowledge your concerns and questions. If you want to get an effective response that is meaningful for both the parties, the preparation becomes vital then.

Host a Dinner Party

Are you new in the neighbourhood and wish to mingle with everyone? You must be looking forward to a get-together where you can meet with your new neighbours and introduce yourself. It can, after all, get lonely to live by yourself if you have entered into a new community. Staying simply with your family all the time might not suffice. You need to become friends with those living around you and get to know their families. In short, your social circle is in need of an upgradation.

Why not simply host a dinner party and send out invites to all the families living around? This can be your chance to mingle with everyone and have an exchange of introductions, as you wished for. For this, you must prepare yourself in advance. It is not just about sending out invites and arranging for food for those people, it is also about you being presentable to all those families you have invited. You need to keep your best foot forward. First impression is the last impression for many. You have to engage with a lot of people hence, you need to give yourself some time to prepare for that mentally. Don't be too hard on yourself. Be warm and welcoming. Keep your personal issues aside for a while and try to be as upbeat and cheerful as possible. You need to cater to the entire neighbourhood after all!

Once families start coming in on the day of the party, be sure to welcome everyone individually. They must feel welcomed in your house. Following the basic party etiquette, ensure that everyone is well-fed and served and nobody feels left out. Engage with everyone in attendance. It can be a tough task but this is what you must do to be able to mingle with everyone. While talking to your guests, let them know how much you appreciate their arrival at the party. Engage in some small talk. It might seem tough to be able to have small talks with everyone around, but that is the need of the hour. You possibly cannot go about introducing yourself for to someone without being an active participant in some small talk. Ask about their families and how have they been doing. You don't have to jump into serious conversation; that, in fact, should be avoided as much as possible for that will keep you occupied for longer than expected with only one guest. And you won't get time to mingle with the others.

To get the conversation going you can question them about the specifics about the neighbourhood like the prevailing security conditions, which nearby school is the best to send kids to, why is there no electricity surprisingly for an hour every other day. Ask them about generic questions that concern you as well as them. Find that common ground and base your conversation on that finding. It should not be a tiresome job to do. Do some of this homework beforehand. Smile and offer a handshake, as and when you meet someone new who you have not introduced yourself to before. Be pleasant. These are the people you are meeting for the first time. There should be no reason for being awful to anyone. In case, the conversation starts to fizzle out, don't hesitate in excusing yourself. Just end the conversation with 'it was nice talking to you. Please help yourself to some desserts.' That's a polite and graceful way of ending your conversation with one group and moving on the next. Plus, no offence would be taken.

While the guests are busy helping themselves to the food and drinks, ensure that none is left out for introduction. Don't stick to one family or an individual for too long. At times, one tends to lose track of time and ends up talking hours on a stretch with that person. Avoid this at all costs. It would be seen as rude and inconsiderate on your behalf if you give all your time to a particular family or an individual and not be able to take out time to meet with others. That would make for some unhappy guests.

Attend Networking Events

If you are trying to get to know more people, attending events like seminars, campaigns for humanitarian causes, books or movies clubs would be a great idea. You would get the opportunity to meet new people there. You will also come across many like-minded individuals. You can make the most of attending such events by mingling with as many people as possible. The mantra is simple—approach them and introduce yourself. If the event that you are attending is a books club, you can actively participate in discussions when you get the chance to. When given the chance, talk about your favourite book and why do you like it the best; you can also discuss works of your favourite author. End your point with an open-ended question that can further the discussion and make it more interesting. It will give others a chance to partake in your conversation and would make for healthy communication. Doing so, you will attract attention of the people present there and that open ways for you to easily network with them. When you have a face-to-face interaction with someone, you get to know how well you connect with them and what are your similarities. This helps you choose whom should you be connecting with.

Note that you should only speak when you get the opportunity to; cutting into another's sentence is a big NO.

There are various benefits of attending networking events. You get to meet the key players of the industry you are interested in and have an inclination towards. Not only do you get to meet them, but also introduce yourself to them. This becomes a good chance to form connections with influential people and get an insight into how they function. This will help you expand your social and professional network. It will also add to your knowledge of how things work in a specific sector. The connections you form here might be of use to you in future or to somebody you know. This is the most crucial benefit of forming strong networks—you can rely on them for professional guidance of any sort in future. People become resources.

Attending such events would help you stay updated on the latest trends in the areas of your interest. You will get to stay abreast of the latest developments taking place in that field. You need not silently sit and grasp all the information being directed towards the audience in such networking events. Participate in the discussions and make your presence felt; cross question, make suggestions, appreciate others for their ideas. Be an active participant. Initiating a conversation with someone at such events can also be a good way to get motivated and inspired; their thought process and ideas might be aligning with yours.

When you are interacting with like-minded people, you open up to new perspectives which can broaden your horizon of understanding things that interest you. For example, if you are attending a workshop on content writing, there could be many new things you would get to know. You might get acquainted with new methods, using which, your content writing can improvise manifold. Attend such events with an open mind and stay open for networking. Be tactical and make use of every opportunity that comes your way to interact with those present.

Talk to Children

Children bring an entirely different perspective even to a mundane topic. Having a conversation with a child can help you analyse situations differently. It is often said that children have a novel way of approaching situations that come their way. There is absolutely no shame and harm in learning a thing or two from them.

The biggest takeaway from a conversation with kids is their positive approach to problems. Unlike us, they do not tend to think of the worst first. They give their best to overcome a hurdle and only when all options are exhausted, they seek help and support. Observe a toddler for example. If their favourite soft toy is lying at a considerable distance from them, they would first attempt to crawl towards it. They would create a fuss and cry only if their attempts of reaching their destination fails—in this case, maybe the soft toy is out of their reach, maybe it is lying on a high table. The point to be noted is that they take the first step on their own.

You can also learn from them how to be imaginative. If you ever find yourself stuck in a tricky situation from where you don't see a way out, think about how a child would deal with the same. One day, you might miss your lunch back at home and there are restaurants for takeaways near your workplace. What would you do? Imagine what a child would do in such a situation. They would share food with others. You can simply walk up to your friends at work and ask about what is 'today's menu'. There is hardly anything to be embarrassed about here. This is what talking to children will bring to you—you will live openly. Overthinking will be obliterated.

Try having a conversation with a child about what would they do if they fail to get their dream job. Their dream job could be anything, right from being an astronaut to being a teacher. You might be in for a surprise once you hear their answers. They are likely to come up with their Plan B. They wouldn't sit and sulk about how wasted their life would feel if they fail to become the one thing they dream of. They would already be ready to have a solution to overcome that 'tragedy'. What does this teach you? It teaches you to be pragmatic and resilient in the face of difficulties that life throws your way. Talk to one and see for yourself. You will be amazed at how different things can seem if looked at from a different perspective.

Children know how to be courageous and not indulge in stressful thinking. They see every day as a new beginning. They look forward to going to school, meeting their friends, playing with them, and studying (though this may not be the same for all kids). They understand what little joys of life are and they cherish those to the fullest. The birds, the morning bell, sun peaking across the window are some of the unparalleled joys of life for them. They know how to wait and admire beauty. We, on the other hand, are always in a rush and end up missing out on such details. Learn how to be calm and positive from them.

It is also true that they express their emotions freely. They say the first thing that comes to their minds and never hold back themselves from working on a thought that crosses their mind. They will convey their ideas and emotions to you in the first go; whether you like it or not is not their concern. They do not care about others' judgements and criticism. It doesn't exist for them. Hence, they are outright fearless in their conduct and approach to things. We, on the other hand, think about an idea twice, or maybe thrice, before uttering it. We are nervous wrecks, unlike them.

Even if you don't have a child of your own, go and talk to those neighbourhood kids and ones of your relatives. Having a hearty chat with them will help you see how they function and approach life. Pick up bits and pieces from their personality and make them yours; implement those in your everyday life. It is not a childish act. There is nothing to lose here. So, embrace their teachings with an open heart and an open mind.

It might not be a very easy job to be able to start a conversation that will have a lasting impact or the one that will be able to serve a purpose and be beneficial. But trying has never hurt anyone.

i. What is it that keeps you going?
ii. How did you manage to survive the emotional loss?
iii. What was the most hopeless moment of your life?
iv. How did you combat your greatest fear?
v. What is the best/worst decision you made in life?
vi. What ails you?
vii. Are you troubled by something on a day-to-day basis?
viii. Do you wish to talk about your hardships?
ix. You and I have a lot in common. Together we can bring about a change.
x. Your experience is invaluable to us.

10

RESPECT ALL VIEWS

*'Without feelings of respect, what is there
to distinguish men from beasts?'*

—Confucius

Imagine talking at a conference and you are suddenly interrupted in between by someone. The person then, all of a sudden, starts pitching in their ideas and viewpoint, dismissing yours. Won't you feel disregarded, disrespected and embarrassed? Such an act would definitely leave you fuming with anger and frustration. It is only human to feel so.

You must have come across people who often tend to make the mistake of putting their thoughts and opinions above those of others. They assign highest value to themselves, not giving importance to what the other person has to offer. They go on about discussing their ideas at lengths, and at times, even intervene in others' conversation to put forth what they think. If possible, keep your distance from such people and stay away from becoming one yourself. Not only is such behaviour making the person appear disdainful, but also disrespectful to others.

While sitting in a group, be it among friends or your colleagues, it is always important that you respect viewpoints of others. It is possible to agree with what everyone has to offer in the group, but even that disagreement can be expressed politely. You do not have to mock and humiliate the other person for expressing their ideas. Any kind of moral or intellectual supremacy should be done away with. Every person sitting there has an equal right to say what they must without any hesitancy. They should be made to feel that they are part of an open-minded group and not one where anything being quoted out of the box is shunned and looked down upon.

Every viewpoint, if given attention to, contributes something or the other to a discussion. The impact might vary, but impactful it is. Hence, you must refrain from discouraging someone from putting forth what they have to say. You might end up learning something new from what you hear; it might be opposite to what you think. Listen to what they say with consideration, keeping an open mind the entire time. You might end up understanding where they are coming from and what is the basis of the thought process. You will end up understanding the person better. Why not give it a try? All you have to do is be attentive when someone is talking about their ideas.

What could be the cause of our ever-dwindling patience with those around us? Why do many of us jump at the first instance of finding any difference between our ideas and those of others? Why don't we just wait for the person to get over with what they have to say and wait for our own turn? This is not a difficult task to accomplish. All you need to do is exhibit respect and consideration for the other person no matter how different their thought process might be from yours. This is basic human courtesy that you ought to practise, remembering how violation of the same would make you feel when you would be targeted. Put yourself in that person's shoes who you interrupted in the last presentation at work. What would have they felt? Think and act.

Encourage Them to Talk

As a teacher, you have asked your students to present PowerPoint presentations on a certain topic, which would be followed by a round of group discussions. Once the students are done with their presentations, you ask them to come forth with questions. What if there is only one child who takes the initiative of participating in the question-answer session? How do you encourage everyone to put forth their ideas and queries?

You can start by asking the students whether they found the presentation interesting. Start by asking open-ended questions. You can ask them to share their views regarding the presentation. First, start the discussion from your end. Tell them which part of the presentation grabbed your attention and why. Slowly, maybe unwillingly, some or the other student is bound to raise their hand to share with the class what they found interesting about the presentation. When the child comes forward to talk, appreciate them for taking the initiative. This will, in turn, also encourage other children to come forward with what they took from today's class. Soon, the enthusiasm will spread among all students and you will have an interactive session. Appreciate the view of every child and thank them on behalf of the class for putting forth their points. Children need such motivation when it comes to public speaking.

Often, the need for such motivation is not limited only to children. Professionals too, can do with some motivation. During a conference, when all of those present get a turn to speak and put forth their ideas, make sure that when it comes to your turn, you should first thank everyone who presented their ideas. Thank them for the inspiration they have brought to everyone in the room. You can even cross-question them on the lines of what they presented. Keep in mind to stay humble as you state your doubts. Asking questions and engaging with the orator would mean that you have paid close attention to what they said, and this in itself is good for boosting anybody's confidence.

Always try to encourage those around you to motivate them for expressing themselves. This will pave way for an interactive conversation where everybody would get to be an active participant. Another way to encourage someone to talk can be by asking for their suggestions and advices on the topic being discussed. In case you know that one of the people sitting in front of you has an expertise on a certain topic, ask them a technical question pertaining to it. This will make them realize that you seek their knowledge. It is a good way to cheer someone and pull them out of their silence.

Listen Well

Work on being a good listener. The better you listen, the better you learn. When was the last time you were mentally present in a meeting at your workplace? Try to listen well this time. Apart from only focusing on what you have to say, include in your sphere of attention, what others have to say too. What they are talking about might be beneficial for you. If nothing, it can add to your knowledge base. Why lose out on an opportunity to grab some useful information? Stop your mind from wandering out the window and focus on what is going on inside the room where you are seated. The person standing in front of you might not be talking about topics that are of entirely direct use to you, but you can always cull out what is of use to you. But for that, you will have to pay attention to what is being said. You might be able to get a clue or a hint for your next assignment, or might get inspiration for a new idea to be proposed. The benefits can be endless.

When someone is discussing about how they plan to execute their idea, pay close attention to it. It is natural for you to have doubts and queries, but do not barge in before they are done talking. You can be thought of as a rude and inconsiderate person. Listen to them to actually comprehend what is being said and not just to be able to throw questions after a few minutes. Free your mind of the purpose of 'listening to debate'. Only after you have done so, will you be able to become a good listener.

As you listen to them talk, maintain your body language in such a way that it shows your engagement with the discussion. Give affirmations to them in the form of head nods and straight eye contact. Not only will this give them the confidence to continue, but will also signify what they are saying is being understood by someone. Don't sit with crossed hands if you are face-to-face with them. It is inappropriate body language for someone who is trying to be a listener. Such a body language can dull the confidence of the person; it will send out a vibe that you are not quite interested in the conversation or you are experiencing some discomfort. This can make the orator feel uneasy.

An effective conversation is inclusive of a sender and a receiver. Listening should not be taken for sitting quietly and with an absent mind. It is a necessity to keep a conversation on track, such that each party gets an opportunity to speak their minds and simultaneously understand what the other is speaking about. You will not be able to decipher what they are talking about if you remain silent, lost in your own world. On the other hand, if you listen to them actively, you will be able to gauge what they are trying to put forth.

Give Reasons for Disagreement

Every conversation is fraught with difference of opinions. Disagreements are natural and inevitable. It is not possible for each member of a group to agree on a certain point at a given time. There will be differences, which later might be obliterated (maybe following coercion) to maintain unanimity. The different opinions arising in a group is a result of diversity—diversity of belief and ideologies. Each person can have their own viewpoint. Before dismissing somebody's take on a topic, the basis of their argument should be understood. While disagreeing with their viewpoint, it should be specified why you are opposing them. The grounds for the discord should be made obvious to everyone.

By stating your reasons for disapproval of their viewpoint, you are making way for a healthy discourse. You can disagree with someone without offending them. The person will be able to get an insight into what made you contradict their viewpoint. It will help them further strengthen their argument or modify it accordingly. This way, your arguments will become productive and not destructive.

Do not disagree with someone on the basis of your personal differences; base it on facts. Remind yourself that it is not the person you are against, it is the ideas they are supporting. Refrain from making personal comments; attacking someone on personal grounds will only lower your image in front of others. They might lose their trust and respect for you. Don't stoop low.

Quote numbers, facts, names and places to explain why you are not on the same page as them. For every disagreement that arises, there should be a logical explanation to back it up. Consider an example as a reference. If your sibling has suggested to not invite certain cousins over a dinner party, ask them why they say so. Then let them know that doing so might create a rift in your inter-personal bonds with them. Your sibling might be having a reason to make such a suggestion. Instead of being cross with them or chastising them, you should simply tell them why you think it will not be a good idea. There is no need for a confrontation. The two of you can sit back and discuss the pros and cons of inviting the cousins over to the dinner party.

You can put forth your point stating your disagreement by saying, 'I am sorry, but I disagree with you about this' or 'I understand where you are coming from, but…' There are polite and humble ways to express to the other person that your views don't align with theirs. As the last resort, why not simply agree to disagree? This will help you put an end to a seemingly never-ending debate in a polite manner. By saying so, you make your stand clear; you communicate to the other person that it is not possible to reach at a consensus as the two of you will never be able to be on the same page regarding the issue.

Drop Sarcasm

The way you put your words can have an impact on what you are trying to communicate. Your tone, accompanying body language and other non-verbal cues can be huge factors in how you are understood. Whether you are complimenting a person or making a comment is often differentiated by a small mark. While the former is based on your genuine admiration for something, the latter is based on your reaction or opinion regarding it. For example, if you like someone's attire, you can compliment them by saying, 'This dress looks beautiful on you', instead of asking 'Where did you get this dress from?' The subject of the focus should be the person and not their dress. Hence, the first remark is more of a compliment than the second. Saying something like 'That is an expensive dress' will be outright sarcastic and penurious at the same time.

Some people use sarcasm as a tool to disarm the other person and rob them of their confidence and motivation. Instead of giving a compliment or even making a productive comment for that matter, they go ahead with throwing in some sarcasm. This is often done in a conversation to gain an upper hand. Sarcasm can be used, based on facts or plain bias. It is used as an equipment for defence mechanism in discussions where you are seemingly losing. If the person is not able to express their real emotions and opinions (in this case, cynical), they resort to using sarcasm. What is often lost on them is that the element of humour and criticism that colours their remark can be emotionally damaging to the one at the receiving end; they can end up being hurt.

It can also be seen as a form of bullying and undermining what the other person expresses in their viewpoint. In case of disagreement, the ideal solution is to give a logical reason for the discord with an argument. Bullying the other and trying to be dismissive about their thought process not only makes for a poor attitude, but also closes all paths leading to a healthy discourse. The other person might or might not be able to decipher the sarcastic tint in the remarks. Either way, they are then prone to be at a loss of words. It should also not be forgotten that sarcastic remarks can often be ambiguous and are likely to elicit no response.

At times, people get habitual of using sarcasm in their everyday conversation under the garb of humour. The usage becomes so extensive that it even becomes unintentional. To avoid forming such a habit, try being cautious of the way you use words while communicating with others. Wait and think before commenting on something; think about how the person in front of you will receive it. Work on your body language and choice of words if you feel that what you are about to say can hurt the other. Make conscious efforts to check your words whenever you have the urge make a comment about something. It's better late than never.

Screaming and Yelling Is of No Use

Trying to get your point across or intercepting someone vehemently just when they are talking serves no purpose in the long run. You might be able to put forth your viewpoint but its gravity will be lost. The essence of your viewpoint will be lost in all the screaming and yelling. Besides, once you stop someone from talking and intervene, you end up leaving a bad impression on others. The communication is dead halfway there itself. Your listeners would lose interest in what you have to say. There is a basic decorum that has to be maintained while engaging in a conversation. Apart from respecting and listening to what the other person is saying, you also have to monitor your own speech and conduct.

At times, the situation might be such that you feel instigated to shout in front of the other person you are having a conversation with. Under such circumstances remember that not giving in to your impulses is what primarily differentiates you from animals. You might feel that you can control that raging anger, but at times, it can go out of hand. Your side of the story will then fall on deaf ears. If you have to ensure that people listen to what you have to say, raising your voice will not make for the best solution. In fact, it is not even an ideal last resort. Instead, maintain your calm even in the face of disagreement and patiently wait for your turn to speak instead of jumping into another's speech.

Consider this example. Conflicts are common in families. Seeing someone in a family lose their cool and yell at another family member is not an uncommon situation. The outcome is also known to everyone. It leads to friction, bickering and dispute and can leave a negative impact on their inter-personal bonds. Yelling in front of children can have long-lasting negative impact on their mental wellbeing. Yelling at children can lead them to have anxiety and stress, which their young minds might not be able to bear.

When it comes to communication, it should be understood that the will to push someone into submission using yelling and shouting will not work. Not only will you break the flow of the conversation, but also create a discord so grave that it would be tough to obliterate it. People will start to avoid talking to you. The worst that can happen is that you become infamous for your bouts of anger. It is bound to ruin your reputation among peers and your seniors.

Keen an Open Mind

Our own biases and set of stringent beliefs keep us from believing and understanding in totality what the other person is talking about. We are so confident and sure of our chain of thoughts that we leave out no space for any new knowledge to seep in. We have forgotten how essential it is to keep our minds open in a conversation. It helps us gain an insight into how the other person functions. This can facilitate your conversation and enrich it, if used the right way.

If you have been a stubborn person all along, being able to open your mind to perceive new viewpoints might be a challenging task for you. Before engaging in any conversation, reflect on what you believe in and why. Focus on the latter. If your reasons seem wise enough to you, ask yourself then the next question which is 'why can you not communicate keeping an open mind?' You might be having your own set of reasons to back up the answer, but don't let that keep you from being able to approach your next conversation with an open mind. When you come across a new set of ideas, question yourself whether they align with your thought process and values. If not, the next question should be why. Give yourself enough time to think. You can also question yourself how is it that the ideas presented can benefit you. Keep aside your bias when doing so. Let the exercise be a genuine attempt at you trying to be permeable enough to your surroundings, and people coming up with ideas that are tad different than yours and challenge you to think.

Try being on a lookout for people who have to offer their unique stand on issues. Study and analyse those. While you do that, keep at bay, your prejudiced thinking and intolerance towards anything novel to you. If you analyse accurately, you will understand where the person is coming from. The basis of their argument might start making sense to you. There is no need to accept what the other has to offer but you should and can show consideration and acknowledgement for the same. In the long run, it might even end up colouring your viewpoint without even you noticing.

You can ask questions about things that are beyond your understanding and cause you to question your beliefs. Ask them what fuels their belief system and ideas. Be humble while you pose questions. Do not do so only to backfire with a premeditated answer or to start an argument. What they tell you should be analysed and tried to be understood. There is nothing in wrong in changing or modifying your viewpoint on the basis of what you hear in a conversation. The end goal for you, of course, is personal growth, and that is only possible if you keep your mind open and flexible to new ideas and thoughts.

Pose Questions Humbly

When questions are asked, a conversation is considered healthy. It shows that you were playing close attention to the speaker. You just have to make sure that those questions are asked the right way and at the right time. Pose your query only when the person is done talking and presenting their stand on a topic. Keep your words simple and to the point. If you make it sound exaggerated and complex, the receiver will not be able to grasp your query and you will be left hanging in mid-air in search for an answer.

Make a suitable choice of words while framing your question. If possible, try to converse in their language. If not for the purpose of social etiquette, it will for sure help the speaker understand your doubts better. Make use of words and phrased used by them in their speech—this will make the question sound direct and more relatable. This will also prevent your question from sounding insubstantial. Before asking the question, reflect on what is the purpose behind it and what is it that you are trying to understand. Plan it well and ask only important questions. It can be possible that your speaker might not be having enough time to cater to all your doubts. Under such circumstances, you should avoid bombarding them with an array of questions. Select the most pressing doubts from your list of questions.

Try to avoid using adjectives and opinions as they are bound to colour your question and might make it appear as a comment instead of a genuine query. So instead of asking, 'What do you think about that terrific idea?', simply ask 'What do you think of that idea?' The latter will be a better way to put it. What you ask should not come across as an opinion and never as a comment intending to insult the intellect of the other. Unless you are a professor or an interviewer, there is no reason for you to question the other in such a way that it tests their intelligence or knowledge base. Question them only for what you need to know and only when you know they will be able to provide you with an apt answer, if not the perfect one.

It should also be remembered that the questions you ask are not just to add to what they have said. That would be called an opinion then. When a talk or conference is opened for discussions, then you may go forth with your opinions.

Everything Cannot Be Seen as Black and White

Not every question you come across will have answers that can be viewed in plain categories of right or wrong. There cannot be just two answers to a question with one being eliminated eventually. The same stands true for arguments made by people; not everything they say can be categorized in the group of acceptable and non-acceptable. There is a grey area. Your work as a listener is to explore the possibility of that space and see how flexible it can be.

When you are hearing someone talk, don't rush towards labelling their words as right or wrong. Opinions, ideas, thoughts—these can be subjective. The option of simply agreeing or disagreeing might not be the right way to approach. At times, there are situations which might not have just a single solution. If probed well, you will arrive at various other solutions for the same. It is natural to be inclined towards following simple and clear-cut rules in one's life, even while making decisions. But it must be realized that there is no unique method that can provide you with the sure shot answer that guarantees your benefit. Whether you realize it or not, you are indulging in a gamble even if you don't know it. The 'safest of your choices' need not turn out to be so in real life when the time comes. Hence, it is always safe to assume all possible courses of action.

As for decision-making, you might argue that it is your personal choice. So be it. But when it comes to a communication, it becomes a matter of being considerate about the other too. Hence, before judging someone and making a comment on their ideas, know that there is no way to ascertain how right or wrong they are. Consider the example of two partners who are on the verge of a divorce. To many, it might occur that the only way out here is a final divorce and separation. Some would agree with giving the marriage a second chance. And there would be some who would suggest to live separately for a while to see how the distance from each another works for them. You cannot criticize a person for opting for any of the three choices as the concepts of right or wrong do not apply here. What they choose can have many reasons behind it, some of which you might not be even able to fathom. So, there is no point in raising a finger on someone on the basis of their choices.

Winning Is Not the End Goal

Unless you are in a debate, winning should not be prioritized as the end goal. When you are part of a discussion, the conversation should be such that it serves the basic purpose of communicating what each of you has to offer without facing any criticism and judgement from either side. The desire to be correct and get acknowledged from everyone often mars the communication. Your attention will not be towards what the other person is saying, but more towards how to put forth your ideas in a superior manner. You will be in a constant battle of trying to belittle the other and prove yourself as the mightier one. Real winning is not about pushing your arguments onto someone as that would only lead to a rift between the two of you; the person will go further away from being persuaded. Winning should be defined as being able to persuade the other person of your point of view by making it compelling enough.

The essence of holding a meaningful conversation will be lost on you. All your focus will then become diverted towards how to discredit others' views. Your inter-personal relationships are put on stake when all you care about is winning an argument. You are not being expected to hold back your real emotions and views. However, express them only with the right words, else you might get into somebody's bad books. Choose to end a discussion with a win-win situation or on neutral grounds. Why would you want to get on the bad side of someone? Take it as a pragmatic or a selfish suggestion—you never know who you might end up needing in your life. There could be many instances where you might need support from someone you once knew. Being able to rely on this person will only be possible if you are in or were in good terms with them. Maintaining strong inter-personal relationships, be it professional or personal, is more important than it is realized to be. A conversation can start to get heated; both the speaker and the listener will begin to lose their ability to understand each other. The mutual respect for each other will be lost.

There should be an exchange of arguments not to win, but to learn. As said earlier, arguments should be based on facts and knowledge, and not on the need to win. You are not taking part in a war where losing would cost you your pride and prestige. It is a conversation that you are indulging in where there cannot be victories and failures. You can, however, be victorious only when you take maximum benefit home from what you hear others talks about; you can fail when you reduce the significance of the conversation to air your pride and belittle the other.

If you have already developed the habit of arguing only for the sake of winning, making changes can be difficult, but not impossible. Whenever you feel the urge to correct someone after hearing their views on a topic, remember that no matter what your professional or social stature might be, you are in no position to chastise anyone for their choices (unless you are a parent) and label them as right or wrong. Don't attach your self-worth to a topic of discussion and argument; you will only end up putting yourself down. The idea should be not to defeat someone but take away a lesson or two from what they share with you. It should be remembered that 'winning' an argument is not about the outcome, it is about the feeling that you want to create for yourself. It becomes a way to soothe yourself into believing that you have the upper hand, while the reality might be entirely different. Jumping to conclusions which are solely based on your viewpoint will bring you no good.

Following are some examples which you can use in your everyday conversations to become more considerate of other people's point of views:

i. What do you think about this?
ii. Do you have any feedback to give on this idea?
iii. What you are saying makes sense, but...
iv. Will you please help us out with this code?
v. Thank you for your views on the subject.
vi. We can really use your expertise, Ma'am.
vii. Can you please explain your point once again?
viii. Can you please give us an overview of the project?
ix. Is it possible for you to make the changes by tomorrow evening? (Drop that sarcastic tone)
x. May I please have your contact number?

11

BRAGGING IS A BIG NO-NO!

'People who boast about their I.Q. are losers.'

—Stephen Hawking

So, your new car has filled you with pride. Is it the second time in the day that you have taken it out for a drive? Be it just to the grocery store? It is after all your dream car which you have been saving for, since the past four years. It is only human to flaunt it right now.

It might be tough for you to think about anything else besides the great mileage that it offers. It might be tough for you to not bring up your new car in every conversation for a few days. Your seemingly never-ending love for it might have started reflecting on your everyday life, unknowingly. Everything else might be seeming secondary right now.

What seems like love for your new car to you might come across as bragging to many in some situations. Knowing this might dampen your mood, but it is true nonetheless. The incessant talk about the same thing might be overwhelming those around you without you being able to notice their frustration. Sharing your happiness with others can very easily turn into bragging about it. So, you need to be cautious. For you, it might be acting as an impetus for your confidence, but eventually, it will start having a negative impact on your inter-personal relationships. They might start avoiding holding any conversation with you for the course of it would already be determined. They are bound to eventually lose interest in talking to you for they would feel that the conversation would eventually be focused on your new car! They wouldn't be entirely wrong in behaving such a manner. Perhaps, it is you who is in need of an attitude shift, and a well thought-out change in your communication pattern. Make the change. There must be many other topics lying untouched to be talked about. There is a world beyond your new car; step into that world. It's time.

The biggest drawback of bragging can be that you will end up being ostracized among friends and family. You are not asked to not share your achievements in life. Share it, laugh and smile about it, shed a happy tear if you must. Then drop it. Not every conversation has to circle around that one achievement of yours. Those who are close to you are happy about it, they are happy whether you continually talk about it or not. Nothing else should matter.

Returning back to the difference between pride and bragging, it should be understood that there is a fine line that demarcates the two. We can often switch from the former to the latter if we don't remain watchful of our behaviour. While pride is a satisfactory feeling about your achievements in life, boasting or bragging is the excessive and unhealthy version of it. Bragging becomes a way of showing off your pride. You let everyone know that you are proud of yourself. This feeling should rather be internalized, instead of being put on public display. Anybody and everybody would despise being around someone who is always boastful of themselves. We can't accuse them for their reaction. Imagine yourself standing in their shoes; imagine you are the one listening to someone talk about 'how tiring travelling to different countries can get every month on business tours' or 'how little you get to relax because you are at the helm of all key responsibilities of the team.' It sure can get tiring and annoying after one point of time. The best you can do is—as said earlier—share your happiness and drop it.

The chapter will delve into how we end up bragging about ourselves (even when unintentional) in conversations and what can we possibly do to avoid this recurring behaviour.

Attracting Attention to Personal Qualities

Maybe you are in complete awe of yourself. The way you approach life and its hurdles instils in you a sense of pride and you cannot help but praise yourself for being able to do so. The worst that you can do is talk about your personal qualities without backing it up with favourable instances. This will be seen not only as a frivolous act, but also excessive self-appreciation; the latter is not to be held synonymous to self-love.

There is no pride in fishing for a compliment and acknowledgment on what you claim or believe is right about you. You should be able to substantiate those claims, else refrain from making those. Not only will people think twice before believing you, the act can also make you look quite shallow. If you do believe that you are exceptional at something, be humble about it. Blowing your own trumpet will serve no purpose and will be of no good to you. Your qualities are of use only to you. If you think those could be put to use for the good of others too, then work on being able to do so. Try not to brag about a selfless act of charity since it defies your reason behind helping them, no matter how noble and selfless it was, to begin with. You should not expect anything in return for the good you have done to others.

If you are financially well-off and often make donations to an old-age home, there is no need to brag about it among your social circle. What can they possibly do with this piece of information apart from applauding you for the same? Remember, they might appreciate your work genuinely. If you are to repeat this story time and again, it would be discarded as just another act of vanity.

There will likely be a difference between your viewpoint and that of your listener. What you see as charity might be viewed as merely your way of giving back to society, which every responsible citizen should be doing any way they deem fit. The two of you might not be on the same page regarding this. Your attempt at gaining appreciation will anyway become a failure then. Give up all attempts to garner the compliments of those around. Just keep on doing what you are good at and what you view as a noble task. That should be enough for you.

The absence of expressing self-love should not be confused with self-depreciation. In no way are you being asked to undervalue or belittle yourself. All you are expected to be is humble, even when it comes to talking about your greatest qualities. Speak of those when you are asked to, like in an interview. Even in an interview, you must weigh your words cautiously. You don't want to come across as a conceited person. Simply list out your qualities in front of your interviewer and do so without embellishing them in anyway. This shouldn't be difficult to understand and follow.

Attracting Attention to Something You Did

You just found out that you have finally aced that interview and landed your dream job. It must be exhilarating thinking about what you achieved and what you have managed to accomplish. All your hard work and dedication finally paid off. You are jubilant with the results and cannot stop gushing about it. You end up calling your parents and close friends to tell them about the exciting news. They are proud of you and congratulate you. Then you decide to post about it on a social media account to let everyone know about your latest achievement in life. There is possibly no one else you can think of who needs to know about this—you suddenly remember the old school friend of yours who had been job hunting previously. You decide to give them a call to share this piece of news.

After the call, you are probably not left as chirpy as you were before. You expected your friend's tone to be more congratulatory. That is likely to dampen your spirits for sure. But there is one thing you are missing out on here. Maybe that friend of yours is facing a hard time still trying to find that job. Hearing you talk about and flaunt your new job, they are bound to feel uncomfortable. Try not to ask about how their job hunting is going. This will make you look inconsiderate; they might not be in the right headspace to be able to talk about. It should be realized that you have reached a stage where you can seek appreciation for your achievement; they are yet to reach there. You talking about it might end up making them feel incompetent.

You need not share everything with everyone. Give some thought before calling up a person or sending out a text to them. There can be various reasons why sharing a happy news on your part might not be the right time. It is possible that they are mourning loss of a family member or have been trying to look for a new home. If you know about their circumstances then reflect and refrain from reaching out to them. You can let them know about it later, when the time is good. The happy news is bound to fizzle out anyway.

Discussing Past Glory

Who does not love reminiscing about the past? Sitting among old friends, colleagues and family members can often take you down the memory lane and that is quite inevitable. Before you know, you would be talking about the merry time you had as kids or how well you fared in that first job of yours. It is not uncommon. Besides, there seems to be no downside to it, no unhealthy touch.

What is seemingly harmless to us has a full potential of blowing up into a narcissist exploration of your 'glorious past'. You should know when to draw the limit between what is acceptable to be discussed and what is not while sitting in a group. You have to be receptive of every person present there. If you have to talk about that job when you were in everyone's good books and had a terrific relationship with your supervisor, first consider who is in your immediate vicinity. If you're sitting with co-workers from your present firm, they can interpret your conversations as boasting. While for you, it might simply be talking about your past experiences, to them, it will become an episode where you are talking highly of yourself as you go on describing what a great people's person you can be. If the worst happens, even your closest friends and family members may become envious of you.

The same goes for discussing the achievements and success stories of your past. Mentioning them casually in a discussion is one thing but going on talking about those at great lengths can be another. At times, the situation might be such that you are expected to do the latter. Even then, do not indulge. State the facts, talk about how that made you feel back then. Dragging it all the way from the past and letting it leave its impact on the way you perceive yourself among your peers or dear ones in the present times might end up causing complications, which will be realized much later. For example, your teammates might be in the need of some instant morale boosting. You being the team manager decide to regale them with your own experiences where you overcome great many hardships with flying colours. Now this can be a tricky situation. You should be able to talk about your past experiences only with the motive of encouraging your co-workers because if the reason is anything else apart from this, your team-workers might end up feeling highly competitive, to the point where they start questioning their own abilities. They should not be forced to draw a comparison between you and themselves. That can be unhealthy for the individual as well as the entire team as a whole.

Did you have a school teacher who was very fond of you and would also appoint you as the class monitor? It must have been very rewarding for you to be acknowledged by your teacher for those timely submissions and project completions. Who wouldn't remember and cherish being praised in front of an entire class? That can definitely add to one's confidence and feelings of self-worth.

As you sit among your school friends after years, you start talking about how honoured you felt back then, when you were appointed as the class monitor. What you are forgetting is that you might be surrounded by people who wanted to have that role of responsibility too, back when you were all young. Hearing you talk about the same may come across as hurtful to them, and in some contexts even rude. There can be numerable examples like these from which we can draw inferences and learn when and how to draw the line when indulging in nostalgia.

One of the easiest ways to be able to stop yourself from indulging in such behaviour repeatedly can imagine yourself to be your own listener. Unless and until you asked for someone to narrate their success stories, would you be okay with them going on discussing about the same incessantly? There might not be many people who would appreciate such an act.

Over-confidence

The lack of confidence or even too much of it, both can be dangerous. The latter stems from excessive belief in yourself. At times, you overestimate your values and ideas believing them to be solely correct and to-the point. This can prove to be harmful in the long run when reality turns out to be different and doesn't meet your expectations.

Being comfortable in your choices and decisions to the point where you wouldn't care to give flexibility even a thought is over-confidence. You become biased with your chain of thoughts and become impermeable to what others have to offer. You come to rely on yourself blindly, not giving thought to the fact that you too can make a wrong move or decision.

It can prove to be damaging to your reputation if not taken care of, before it is too late. Being confident and self-reliant can take you places; the same is not true, however, for over-confidence. There is one distinction between a confident and an over-confident person—while the latter always have a need to boast about themselves, the former don't carry such habits.

A simple example of being over-confident can be arriving late for a meeting. Maybe you did the calculation; you calculated the distance and the time it should take to cover that. Maybe you even considered coming across traffic on your way to work to attend the early meeting. You feel confident about making it to your office right on time. So, you leave at 8 to be able to reach by 9. It is just a one-hour journey after all, if you take the shortest route available. However, by the time you arrive for the meeting, it is 9.30 already and you have disappointment written all over your face. Perhaps, the shortest route you were relying on was blocked for a construction work which started on the same day. You may call it bad luck, but the fact cannot be ignored that you should have aimed to reach the place half an hour early. Being confident about being able to reach on time only ruined your flexibility in adopting a different schedule.

You should be able to see the potential drawbacks of your beliefs and perspectives. It is important to be prepared for varied outcomes and not fixate on one. Over-confidence can also be a by-product of stubbornness. Being stubborn makes you blind to any inconsistencies or lapses in your plan of action. You stick to it thinking it to be the most fool-proof plan there ever could be. This is only the first downside of being over-confident. The other is that, surprisingly, it can hamper your growth and performance in various aspects of life.

When you become too sure of yourself, you tend to become relaxed and a little laid-back in life. It should be realized that a bit of nervousness and self-doubt is imperative to bring about a sense of caution in your work which will helps you do your best. Once you are no longer at your guard, you run the danger of losing in a particular situation. For example, you are sure of being able to complete a project before its deadline and are under the impression that the time given is more than sufficient. Hence, you start working at a sluggish rate, thinking you will easily turn in your project on time. The result turn out to be much different from what you had anticipated—you ended up missing the deadline. This will definitely leave you astonished as well as disappointed because you were rooting for the opposite, and were thus totally unprepared for such an outcome. Your over-confidence ended up costing you your task performance.

Having confidence in yourself can help you stay motivated and on top of your game. It will help you become independent and rid you of any self-bashing tendencies you might be harbouring. A mere excess of the same can take you in the opposite direction. Over indulgence can take you away from the objective accuracy of your judgements, the judgements you made on the basis of your subjective confidence.

Give Credit Where It's Due

It is never acceptable to not give someone their due credit. This should be taken as a mantra to be followed, not only when working in a group, but also when you are working by yourself. While you might be working alone on an assignment, often there are people in the background whose constant support help you to channel your energies and set the right foot forward. Why not give them a credit for their unconditional support? Sharing credit of your success should not be viewed as a difficult thing to done. All you have to do is give acknowledgement to them. Let the person know that you are thankful for how they facilitated in helping you reach where you are. It could be anyone, from your parents to your spouse. Apart from them, let others who stood beside you in tough times know that you appreciate them too.

At work, there might be a few interns working under you helping you in finish the project before the deadline. Give them their credit, no matter how small their efforts were. Not only will they appreciate this gesture of yours, but it will also help them stay motivated on the professional front. An acknowledgement will convey that no contribution to the team goes unnoticed and unappreciated. They will remember this in the long run. It is always encouraging to receive compliments for what you have accomplished and how. A small 'you did a great job', or 'your presentation was perfect' are easy to give compliments and you never know when such a praise might end up brightening one's day. It also becomes a mark of the fact that you appreciate sincere and hardworking people, regardless of their experience or designation.

When working within a team, a situation might arise when you alone are lauded for the project which is also being taken care of by three other colleagues. You should go ahead and humbly accept the praise, bringing it to everyone's attention that the project has been a team-work and you couldn't have managed to complete all of that on your own without your colleagues' contribution. Talk about how you all have worked together to make the project a success. Even when you are lauded for the work on a one-on-one basis, give others their due credit. Wanting all the limelight and accolades for yourself will be ethically and professionally wrong. Besides, sooner or later, everyone would know who all pitched in for the project.

There might also come a time when you come up with an idea but its inspiration is someone else whom you know. There is no harm in admitting to this fact. You should let people know how you came up with the idea. That might even make for an interesting story to tell. If nothing else, it will clear your personality of any conceivable vanity.

Extend Your Support

Nothing good comes out of jealousy—this is something that many people have preached across ages, and it still stands true. Just like that new car is a reason for you to celebrate, a new house might be the reason to celebrate for others. While you go on talking about that car to your friends and family, they might be doing so too. There is no difference. Your car has been your success story and to them, it has been their new house. Instead of being jealous of what the other has achieved, you should be happy for them, regardless of whether they were equally content for you. Being happy for someone is not part of barter system wherein you must give something only on receiving. Shower them with your support, let them know that you are happy in their happiness. Join in the celebrations.

Do not let feelings of envy and bitterness creep into your mind. That will inhibit you from being able to extend any support. If you are only happy in the moments of your own successes and fail to express the same for others, people might start ignoring you—it might seem pointless to be associated with someone who would not partake in their happiness and praise them for their achievements. If you cannot actively participate in their happiness, be sure to not spoil it for them. Refrain from being too inquisitive about the details. Questions like 'how much did you pay', 'what all options did you have' might not sound very appropriate in the moment.

You should not fall into the trap of drawing comparisons. It is never productive and can only give way to negative thoughts. Aspire for greater things and not because the other has achieved them. You can always appreciate and admire how one is leading their life, but do not start associating your misery to their growth. The two are not linked together. If not done so, it will become a thirst which will be impossible to quench. You will always find yourself in a state of lack, always wanting something that the other has. This will ensure a perpetual state of longing. While no justification needs to be given for saying this, it should be noted that everyone finds growth in life at their own pace and nothing is too fast or too slow. What has happened to others is perhaps not meant to happen to you and vice-versa. Your best friend is a mother by 30. That should not become a reason for you to sit back feeling despondent about not having a child of your own. This should not become a scale for you to gauge how far you have come in life. Having a child should not become a parameter for measuring your happiness. Maybe you have different things to plan ahead, motherhood can wait for the time being. Even if you are not at peace with how things are going on in your life, looking on how others are faring might not be a good motivator to start with. This will only end with you harbouring jealousy and you might not be able to appreciate things like before.

Might Attract Negative Vibes

Once you go on talking about how content your new job makes you, you attract attention—good and bad. There will be some who will be glad for you and would wish you all the luck. Then, there would be some who might express happiness on the outside but from the inside, would be tired and annoyed listening your stories. It might be possible that you have unintentionally ended up shifting the entire party's focus on yourself and your new job. It is not possible to spend an evening of merry-making by discussing about one person's professional life. This will very likely irritate many of those present around you. The grounds are justified. Imagine yourself in their shoes for once. What would you do if you expected and hoped to be able to relax for an evening and forget about an aspect of your life but you are still forced to think about it? Won't you too be irritated with the person who started the conversation in the first place? They might even end up withdrawing and excusing themselves from the conversation on one pretext or the other.

With your listeners leaving the conversation—or rather your monologue—you are bound to feel surrounded by some negative energy. It is a no-brainer. This negative energy will be encompassing the jealousy or the irritability that you have induced. You might notice them rejoicing with you initially, but their vibes would give them away. It would cause repulsion. Such vibe is bound to cause you immense discomfort. You will find that they are alienating themselves from you.

To avoid such situations, you should know when to stop talking and how much information to divulge in a conversation. Set your boundaries. Learn to control what you utter, rather what you choose to. Learn the distinction between the two. You might have shared the happy news of your new job unknowingly and without any intention to the grab attention of those around you; there is also the possibility that you chose to talk about your new job to be able to boast about it openly. The latter might be tolerated in the name of social etiquette for a while, but you will end up getting on their bad side.

It might not be your intention to raise anyone's hackles at the get-together, but it ended up being so. You can now stop talking about that new job before it ruffles someone's feathers again.

Be an Empath

You can stop being someone who brags. All you have to do is learn how to be an empath. Try to analyse a situation from the other's perspective. This will help you understand why do they or don't prefer something you have said. You may have cracked a joke at their expense in a gathering or you may have ridiculed them for their choices under the veil of humour. The reasons can be endless.

Imagine yourself at a birthday party where you meet some of your long-lost family members. While engaging in conversation with each of them, you ask them questions about how they have been all this while. For every question you ask, you give them an update on your life regardless of whether they ask you about it or not. This doesn't stop for hours. By now, you have told them about the NGO you started, how you collaborated with a school as part of a campaign for right to education for all, and even how good you are at gardening! They surely know much more about you than you know about them. Maybe they didn't get a chance to divulge much. It is possible that they already have formed an opinion about you by now. It might not be a good one given the way you carried on with the conversation.

They are bound to make assumptions about you on the basis of the information you gave. The matter can become even more unfavourable if one of them has been trying to do something of a similar sort in their career, but have failed miserably time and again. This person might start believing that you're boastful and conceited. Even if you did not intend to hurt sentiments, it is always better to keep a check when it comes to talking about yourself. Your over-enthusiasm for telling your experiences can be mistaken for bragging very easily. This can even become a frequent occurrence if you do not change your ways.

Before talking about yourself with others and sharing your life experiences, it is better to know as much as possible about the person first. Give them a fair chance to talk about themselves. That will make for an ideal conversation. Doing so will give you an insight of the ups and downs faced by the them in their life. With such information, you can moderate what you talk about ensuring that nothing hurtful or disrespectful is said. You could have thus refrained from putting forth information about your professional life, had you taken proper initiatives to know more about that relative of yours.

At times, you might end up bragging about your accomplishments in front of someone to whom it may seem nothing short of a dream or an unachievable task. This can cause hurt to that person. That new car might be a dinner table topic for you, but for someone you are talking to, it need not be so. Their focus can be rather on how to get food on their table next month. There are so many differences in the world. There will be examples of such inequalities in every community or social group to which you belong. Instead of closing your eyes to such duality, you should acknowledge it. Recognize that it is present in the lifestyle choices that people make or are forced to make. That will be your first step towards becoming an empath. Not only will it help you become an empath, but also open up wider understanding of what an ideal conversation entails.

By now, you should be aware of what all should you avoid

saying if you don't want to come across as someone who brags. You can read these 10 instances to understand why these won't be received well.

  i. I was the first one to come up with this idea.
  ii. Guess how much I bought my new car for?
  iii. This dress was hand-made in Italy.
  iv. Have you seen my new phone? It comes with the latest technology.
  v. Let me show you my china set. It is an antique.
  vi. Don't you just love the design on this carpet? I chose it.
  vii. The leather of this bag is so fine. I insist on going for the real deal.
  viii. We went to Paris for a trip. We had a blast.
  ix. The children are getting a PS5 this Christmas.
  x. We plan to travel to throw a party again this New Year's—bigger and better!